Barney's Knob

Also by Laura Larsen

Facing The Final Mystery: A Guide to Discussing End-of-Life Issues

Barney's Knob

A Memoir of a Time and Place

LAURA LARSEN

Blue Sky Press
Klamath Falls, Oregon 97601

BLUE SKY PRESS
341 Hillside Avenue
Klamath Falls, Oregon 97601

Copyright © 2019 by Laura Larsen

All rights reserved. This book may not be reproduced in whole or in part, stored in a retrieval system, or transmitted in any form or by any means — electronic, mechnical or other — without written permission from the publisher, except by a reviewer, who may quote brief passages in a review.

Library of Congress No. 2019912586. Cataloguing-in-Publication data is available.

Design & Typography: Susan Dworski/The Blue One
Cover Art: Marjorie Muns
Author Photo: Elissa Kline

First Printing, September 2019
ISBN 978-0-578-56016-8
eBook ISBN 978-0-578-57518-6

Printed in the United States

This is dedicated to Ray.
His support sustained me.

ACKNOWLEDGEMENTS

Thank you to all my family and friends for making this happen,
the book and my life on Barney's Knob.

Readers
Trudy Way, Carolyn Han, Perri Zepeda, Teresa Rennick

Book Design & Layout
Susan Dworski

Editing
Amanda Dworski

Cover Art
Margie Muns

Contents

BEFORE THE KNOB • 1963-1968

The Letter 1963	1
The One Arrives 1963	3
We Become Acquainted 1963-1965	7
We Get Married 1965	10
Autumn Winds 1966	14
Travels 1967	16

LIVING ON THE KNOB AS CARL'S WIFE • 1968-1984

First Visit to The Knob 1968	21
Letting in the Light 1968	24
Carole 1968	26
The Aftermath 1968	30
John Erik 1968	34
Rain 1969	37
The Screen Porch 1969	39
Ruthann 1970	42
Fire 1970	45
Baubles & Bangles 1971-1973	48
Neighbors 1971-1973	50
Tom & Tasha 1971	56
Wood 1971	60
Swen 1972-1973	64
Yoga & Toni 1973	68
Moving Next Door 1974	71
Blue Sky 1974-1979	75
Cultural Adventures 1975-1985	80
Ideas Brewing 1975 and on...	87
Bob & Carol & Ted & Alice 1975	91
Encinal Canyon 1976	97
Boy-San 1977	99
Holistic Health 1978 and on...	103

Personal Fire 1978	107
Wildfire 1978	110
Paddle Cats 1978-1982	113
The Seminal Weekend 1981	119
Writing & Dancing 1982-2006	123
Home School & Heartlight School 1982-1983	126
The Undertoad 1983-1984	131
The Mistaki Club 1984	133

LIVING ON THE KNOB AS CARL'S NEIGHBOR • 1986-1999

Tom to the Rescue 1984	139
Gina & The Hermes Project 1985-1987	143
Living Next Door	148
Helpers 1985 and on...	151
Travel Helped, Too! 1985 and on...	158
Over the Fence 1986	161
Divorcing 1986-1989	165
Elissa 1989 to the present	171
Divorced 1989	175
Many Changes 1989	179
Workshops, Gale, Travels, Heart Openings & Closings 1990-1997	182
Facing the Final Mystery 1997 to the present	187
Lois 1998	189
One Last Trip to Denmark 1998	191
Leaving The Knob 1999	195

AFTER THE KNOB • 1999-2018

Creating a New Life 1999 to the present	203
Swen's Wedding 2007	208
Carl and I Talk, Sort of... 2007	212
Carl and I Hug, Sort of... 2010-1011	215
The Final Days 2012	218
Epilogue 2018	222

Before The Knob

1963 - 1968

The Letter

1963

I was turning twenty years old when the letter arrived. Apparently, my high school pal, Barbara, never forgot my longing for a romantic and kindred spirit. In November 1963, I received a three-page, single-spaced typewritten letter from her. In it she described a tall, handsome, Viking-God-like guy named Carl whom she had met at Glendale College the previous year. They were in a group that discussed "important topics," such as population control, religion, Kerouac and Ginsberg and cultural changes at hand. She knew this man was right for me, but she was not in the mood for sharing him at that moment.

The next fall Barbara had moved on to Whittier College, and Carl had started taking classes at Santa Monica College. Since he was living close to me geographically, she composed the letters of introduction; one to me and one to Carl.

"He is so rare, to be so handsome and yet so interested in philosophical and spiritual issues," she wrote. "He is like a rough diamond that needs polishing!" Well, I was certainly capable of doing that and had been waiting for the opportunity.

She also typed, "He will always take the hard road rather than the easy one in his search for meaning."

That could be a red flag, but what the heck.

Further, Barbara noted, "Carl has had quite a past, so be mature if he tells you his stories." He was only twenty-two, so what kind of past could he have? And besides, I had been craving stories for a long time, especially those that were not about cars, college classes or fraternities, which was all I heard from the college boys I had dated.

The day after I received the letter, I found my cotton-candy-spinner pal, Sheila, and asked her to get the same lunch break as mine. We had started working at Pacific Ocean Park (POP) on weekends at the same time and discovered we had the same romantic dreams of finding a unique man, the likes of which neither of us had met. Yet.

"I have news to share and it is important!"

She found me sitting on the pier's edge with my feet swinging, munching my jack cheese and green apples. We had discovered that was a favorite lunch for both of us.

"Listen to this! I got it in the mail yesterday from a high school friend."

As she got her lunch out, I read the letter to her. She seemed to fall into the same swoon and have the same heart palpitations that I had. Could there be such a guy? She hugged me and begged me to keep her posted. What happened next was that he called me and made a date to see me the following Sunday.

The One Arrives

1963

I was living at my parent's apartment in Santa Monica. The doorbell rang. I opened the front door and was looking at a pair of knees. Carl was standing on his hands, his charming smile already drawing me in, even if it was upside down. Momentarily, the smile was upright and even more engaging, because it turned up at the corners as if he were a very tall elf. Bright, sparkling blue eyes. He had a crew cut, which was my least favorite hairstyle—hardly the Spanish poet look—but there was a light in his eyes that I had never seen, the light I had been waiting for that projected familiarity and connection.

I swallowed the drool I had produced while gaping at his imposing presence.

"Uh, come on in," I stammered.

Introductions were made, and we discussed the La Crescenta connections with my mother's cousins, Harris and Lenore, who were visiting. Lenore turned out to be Carl's fifth grade teacher. This seemed like a good sign that he was already not a total stranger. The vibes were good, even though I am sure I did not know what "vibes" were at that time.

My mother had left her purse at the restaurant where we had eaten, and Carl gallantly offered to retrieve it, so we set off on phase one of our first date. In fact, our first topic of conversation centered on how much we both disliked dating. This thrilled me.

"I hate having to dress and behave in a certain way," I said. I had given up wearing girdles but didn't mention that. He agreed, "It's just too formal. I can never think of anything to say."

Carl led me to his car, a 1957 Ford convertible—currently not convertible—since there was no top or windshield. He explained the missing parts.

"I was in Mexico recently and driving at night. I suddenly saw planks of wood jutting into the road from the back of a truck. I held on tight to the steering wheel and ducked and when I sat up again, the roof and windshield were gone. At least my own head was still attached!"

Wow. I was glad he ducked and lived to tell the story. I also mused that I couldn't imagine myself on a dark and unfamiliar Mexican road.

We drove to the Marina in all that fresh air and found my mom's purse. He then turned east on Jefferson Boulevard and said, "So move over here," patting the center of the front seat. I eagerly slid over. It was definitely easier to hear each other, given the vast width of the vehicle's front seat and the roaring wind. I liked sliding up next to him. It made me smile but I looked away, almost embarrassed at feeling so comfortable and happy.

Only a few blocks had passed by when he remarked, "So, what's that hole in your jaw?" If I had not already been bedazzled by his grin, the spiritual eye-sparkles and the instant ease I felt with a male person, I would have wanted to hide under the seat when he noticed my deformity. No one had mentioned it in several years, so I assumed I had done a good job of hiding it.

When I was fifteen, I underwent surgery on a lump under my jaw. Once the incision healed and the bandages were removed there was indeed a gaping dent in my left jawbone, not to mention that when I opened my mouth, my lower left lip moved right inside my mouth, unless I manually held onto it in order to chew. This was an awkward activity, since Bob's Big Boy hamburgers were a frequent dietary necessity.

Anyway, five years had passed. The nerve damage had slowly healed so that I was able to eat a hamburger without tugging on my lower lip. I still tilted my head to the left and down and it is a wonder that my cervical spine did not freeze in that direction. The hole in my jawbone became a dent and hardly noticeable, or so I thought.

Instead of turning red and mumbling, I laughed and looked directly at him. He laughed. It was good. This was the first of his efforts to be comfortable with me that evening. He was bold and forward, and I liked it.

He pulled into a bowling alley on Jefferson Boulevard and we ordered tea, the first of many cups that evening.

"I want to get this out of the way," he began, and then told me the main scenes of his past that Barbara had mentioned.

"When I was fifteen, I ran away to Florida with my girlfriend, Dee, who was seventeen. We sort of borrowed my family's second car and some cash."

Okay. Be mature.

"We stayed for about six months, me working in a welding shop and she as an exotic dancer. And then we found out she was pregnant. We called home. They encouraged us to return, despite how worried they had been during those months. They helped us find an apartment and insisted we get married. We did.

"The baby was born. Three weeks later, we found the baby in her crib, dead. Dee was wild with grief. It seemed the only way to calm her was to try for another baby. A boy was born. We named him Carl, Jr."

Wow. This was no small stuff to deal with as a teenager.

He continued, "We were not able to get along. We fought all the time. I joined the Navy with my best friend, Frank, and the marriage gradually fell apart when the boy was less than two years old."

My mind was doing the math. He was still only nineteen by the time all of this happened.

"I found my clothes and stuff out on the porch one day when I came home, and that was that. I felt devastated and free at the same time. I visited the boy one time and then didn't see him again. I heard that Dee had remarried."

When it was my turn to tell my history, I had little to say. Two doting parents, nice home, good friends. I was in college studying to be a nurse. I liked to read. Ho hum.

Carl drove up into Brentwood where he was living in a work/exchange-for-board situation, at the home of a sprightly octogenarian, Mrs. T. He was not allowed to have lady visitors so I was instructed to get onto my hands and knees and crawl past Mrs. T's windows. I saw this as more of the new adventure.

Inside the quaint garden apartment attached to the main house, I saw his book collection, a self-portrait in clay…*ah, an artist for sure*…and two rooms that were tidy. I guess he learned housekeeping during his four years in the Navy.

There was a single bed. He stretched out on it and motioned me to join him. Once I lay next to him he slung his leg over my legs. I snuggled against him and felt I had gone to heaven. We continued exchanging our stories. Later when I had to use the bathroom, he called out, "I can hear you peeing!" I knew this was a further attempt to feel comfortable.

He drove back to my parents and followed me up the stairway.

"What's that all over your butt?" I stretched my head behind my shoulder and saw circular purple blobs all over my backside. The topless Ford had been parked beneath a pittosporum tree, which had dropped its berries onto the seat. On a "normal" date, I would have been embarrassed. I was not.

I knew he was the one!

We Become Acquainted

1963 – 1965

Our courtship began. The first week was a big one. JFK was assassinated. I was on my way to the college cafe to tell my friend Ruthie that I had fallen in love. The loudspeaker blared the tragic news. It felt ironic that as my life was beginning, another had ended. I didn't know what to say to Ruthie. We remained silent, listening to the updates.

My school, UCLA, and Carl's, SMCC, were closed for the next few days. We found each other and drove out to Leo Carrillo Beach. We sat in one of the caves snacking on a bottle of orange juice and a can of Spanish peanuts, sharing our goals and dreams. He wanted to be an artist, a writer or a philosopher...he wasn't sure which. I wanted to be a nurse. Period. Nothing else had formed in my young mind by that time.

He came over one night and had dinner with my dad and me. My mom worked nights. It went well. Another day for breakfast with both my parents. My mom was delighted that he was tall with blue eyes, instead of the swarthy types I had been drawn to since junior high.

On Thanksgiving weekend, I met his parents, who had divorced when Carl was eighteen. His mother, Virginia, was now married to Don. Carl's sister, Carole, was fourteeen at the time. The next day I met his father, Eric, who was now married to Alice. Alice had a daughter, Karen, who was also fourteen. Carole had to meet her dad outside when he came to pick her up because Eric and Virginia didn't speak to each other. No one in my extended family on either side had divorced, so this was an eye-opener.

One spring day, Carl dropped me off at school. I was so smitten by this time that upon waving goodbye to him, I walked smack into a cement pillar...good thing my head was turned toward him or my nose would have been broken.

We handwrote long letters to each other, even though we lived in adjoining towns. There was so much depth and connection, which I had never felt before, despite my loving parents.

A week later, I met Frank. He and Carl had been best friends since the age of ten. Both of them had jobs that provided living arrangements in exchange for chores. Frank taught swimming to a family's children. Carl shoveled manure at the home of Mrs. T.

The following summer, at the Ford Theater to see "King Lear," we met Frank with his new girlfriend, Patsy. He had described her to us as "the girl with the green shoes." She and I recognized each other—we had attended the same high school, though did not have classes together.

Troubles brewed at Mrs. T.'s. Her grandson, Ralph, lived next door with his parents and sister. Ralph adored Carl and tried to spend as much of his free time with him as possible. They played guitars together, and Carl told him about books he was reading for his Western Civilization class. Somehow, Ralph's parents decided Carl was a Communist and told Mrs. T. she must ask Carl to leave. She did, though told him he could live in her beach house out in Malibu and sweep the leaves for his exchange. (Ralph had managed to hitchhike the fifteen or so miles to reach Malibu...what to him was his real education).

Meanwhile, my mom's initial appreciation of Carl faded. She didn't like that he wore sweatpants with holes in the knees, that we liked to drink tea and burn incense instead of going out dancing, plus the fact that his parents were divorced. Her reactions broke my heart. I couldn't make her understand that this was the most important experience I had ever had and that I would not stop seeing Carl. He was dangerous in her made-up opinion.

I Move to Mrs. T.'s

In the fall, I moved into the little garden apartment at Mrs. T's in exchange for rubbing her legs and arms each night before she went to sleep—perhaps a precursor to my later becoming a massage therapist. No men were allowed, so now Carl had to crawl on the pathway to my rooms.

My school semester continued.

Our romance continued.

And then, just before Christmas, Mrs. T. found out that Carl was visiting, and so was Ralph.

I had to go.

We Get Married

1965

Carl and I discussed the possibilities. Living with classmates wasn't an option. I wasn't going to move back to my parents'. I couldn't live with him in sin—we were barely out of the fifties. The logical solution was to get married! Carl had quit school after Mrs. T. helped him get a job on the sport fishing boats at Malibu Pier. He had built an eight-by-eight-foot plywood box inside a building at the foot of the pier where he was living. He had a bed, typewriter and more orange juice and Spanish peanuts. We found a duplex at the foot of Topanga Canyon, half-way between UCLA and the pier.

We told my parents we wanted to see them. It was the Tuesday before the New Year, 1965. When we shared our exciting news of getting married and that we had found a duplex, my mother looked like I told her I had cancer. My dad was neutral. We thought we would do it at semester break, a month away, to give us all time to prepare.

My mom said, "Why don't you get married now? You can have the wedding here." Well, okay, that was fine with us, though I always thought it was because she was afraid we would have sex in the duplex before getting married. Of course, we were already having sex, as often as possible.

The plans began. Sunday, January third was selected. Carl and I ended up running to the Santa Monica City Hall with our blood test reports—no syphilis—at 11:45, just before it closed down for the rest of the long holiday weekend. We met with the Presbyterian minister from my parents' church, who asked me, "Did you realize Carl had already been married?" As if we hadn't talked personally yet! "Of course, I know that," I retorted almost angrily. Carl was silent. He was suspicions of organized religion. A restaurant was chosen, by my mom, for the dinner. A smattering of longtime family friends was invited. I forgot to invite my best friend at the time, Vieva. I asked my high school pal to be my maid of honor, because we had pledged to be that for each other when we were sixteen. I later felt sorry that I had not asked Barbara to be my witness since she introduced Carl and me. At least I remembered to invite her. I spent the last night at my parents.' My mom's parting advice was, "You are throwing your life off a cliff."

The ceremony was okay. I wore one of my multiple bridesmaid dresses and dyed-to-match pointy-toed shoes. Carl rented a white sport's jacket from somewhere. Patsy took photographs, since Frank was best man. We got through it and moved onto the restaurant. My mother had ordered a cake, and because of the holiday weekend, there was no delivery service from the bakery. She put the cake on the back seat of her Rambler, and when she swerved around a corner, it tipped upside down onto the floor…smashed roses and all. I often wondered if it was a way she could quietly express her anger and fear. It all seemed as if a haze hung over the day's activities. We returned to my parents' apartment and opened gifts, packed them up and drove to the duplex in our twin Renault Dauphine cars. I am guessing we were too tired to have sex, at least I don't remember it. The next day, I went to school and Carl went to work. My classmates were surprised at my announcement! So was I.

I continued at nursing school, rotating through pediatrics and psych. Carl continued on the boats with one of the old salts helping him to get an Ocean Operator's License. He had the talent to drive the boats and the interest to do so. The only thing he lacked was the required five-year's experience. Somehow, that was passed over.

In September, we heard about a mountain cottage in Corral Canyon. It was tiny but had a fireplace and a view of the canyon and the ocean beyond. We had to step through a window in the living room or go outside to get into the bedroom through the door, as the bedroom was wall-to-wall windows. It was magical to wake up and feel as though we were outdoors, yet warm and toasty.

At Christmastime, the cottage was sold and we were told to pack up. I begged the landlord to let us stay through Christmas. He agreed. Carole stayed with us, and we all got new jammies for gifts and wore them for four or five days. Patsy and Frank visited. They were planning their wedding.

We were sad to leave the mountain cottage, but we moved up in the world, finding a home on Bonsall Drive with fifty peach and apricot trees, grape vines, a stunning canyon for hiking and only a few blocks from Zuma Beach. It was in probate for a year after the owner had died. We dealt with his dentures next to his bed and bodily fluids on the sheets. We found boxes of correspondence between him and his wife, while he was in the Merchant Marines. A nephew was the heir and had no interest in the estate except to sell it. We felt we were the sole witnesses to his life, since he had no children.

The house itself was one large room surrounded by windows, overlooking the orchard. There was a large kitchen with glass doors on the cupboards that were outlined by Scandinavian-style painted borders. Morning glories draped over the window next to the kitchen table.

Patsy and Frank's wedding took place in a stone church in La Crescenta, with a lively reception filled with Serbian food, music and dancing—much different than our wedding day.

I graduated from nursing school in January 1966 with an outdoor ceremony and caps and gowns. I stayed at UCLA Medical Center on the same floor of my last rotation. My patients were very ill with terminal kidney disease and hopeful transplants. Many remained on that floor the whole year I was there.

I took the Nursing State Boards, and whereas my classmates were receiving their results, I was not. I rushed to the mailbox every day, and finally...there it was. I had flunked! The only one in my class! I was devastated and sobbed and sobbed until Carl got home. The next day I met with my OB teacher, Mrs. Kades. She taught the section I had failed. I adored her and sobbed some more. She said, "Remember, that was the semester you met Carl. I am sure your attention was elsewhere!" It was, and I appreciated her reminding me. I had to remove my RN pin at work. It was humbling to say the least. Sometime in the spring, Carl and I took a little vacation in Long Beach, where I was able to take the boards again. This time I passed.

One day I arrived at home and was too tired to get out of my VW Beetle. A throwaway newspaper was on the ground beside my car, and I picked it up and thumbed through it. In the classified section was an ad which read: Part Time RN for family practice in Malibu. I thought, no more commuting, no chronically ill and dying patients. I raced up the stairs and called the posted phone number. The next day I was interviewed and got the job. I gave notice, and in two weeks I was driving ten minutes instead of almost an hour to work in a converted house with tangerine trees outside every window. My boss was Dr. Hodges. His mother Gert was the secretary. There were two other RNs, Smokey and Margaret, so between us, there were always two RNs available each day. Bob was the night-man during the week and stayed in what had been the living room and kitchen of the house to receive the emergencies after hours. It was like having a new family right away. Regular patients came in for appointments, and if there was an accident or incident in Malibu, the ambulance brought the patients to us. Thus, we had both calm days and exciting days.

    It was perfect.

Autumn Winds

1966

Our friend Mike, who owned the local dive shop, called one day and asked if he could bring an interesting customer over for dinner. He thought we would enjoy his exotic company. "Of course," we said, always appreciative of stimulating conversation and someone new to meet.

"This is Edmundo Edwards," Mike said, introducing us to a slender and stooped young man, with a scraggly beard and bright brown eyes. "He's from Chile and is here selling his father's pre-Columbian pottery collection to gather funds to make a trip to Easter Island."

I looked at Carl and noticed his interest piquing. He loved the word island, and we had talked about his yearning for adventure, which was not assuaged by being in the Navy. He was sent to Kansas, while Frank went to Japan.

"*Con mucho gusto*," said Edmundo. I went into the kitchen to prepare dinner. I could already see our lives changing without any more words being spoken. By the time we finished dinner, Edmundo had told us that his grandmother owned and managed the largest newspaper in Santiago. He had a ship of some sort to make the journey, which needed repairs, and had already gathered a crew of an Argentinian, Frenchman and Easter Islander to participate in what he called Expedition Haumuana. He mentioned that Carl would be an ideal crewmember, since he had an Ocean Operator's License, never mind it would not be viable in Chilean waters.

After Mike and Edmundo left, Carl and I talked.

"What would you think if I decided to do that?" he asked me. I wasn't stunned, because I could see it happening before my eyes. But I wasn't pleased or excited for him either.

What would our parents think? And our friends?

We were only twenty-three and twenty-five at this time, so still connected to our parents. We had barely been married for two years. Wasn't he supposed to still be madly in love with me and not want me out of his sight? We agreed to think about it for a few days. Our time in the peach orchard would be up at the end of the year, so that change was already in the making.

I found a William Blake poem that provided some inner comfort:

> *He who binds himself to a joy*
> *Does the winged life destroy*
> *But he who kisses the joy as it flies*
> *Lives in Eternity's sun rise*

We made the decision for him to go. Our parents were as appalled as I expected them to be. And yet, my own father had returned to Denmark for a year in the middle of his courtship with my mom, which seemed similar to me, but not to her. Granted they were not married, but still….

I asked Carl to hold off until after Christmas. We celebrated with our families, and the day after Christmas, I drove Carl to the Santa Monica Greyhound bus station to make the first leg of the journey to Mexico City.

Once the bus pulled away, amidst tears from both of us, I drove to Palisades Park with my new companion, Coco. Our friends Stuart and Ursula had found this standard, untrimmed poodle and thought he resembled Carl with his reddish curly hair and would be good company for me. He was. We walked in the park, me crying, Coco at my side. Once back at our home, I began packing our belongings, which were not many, and prepared to move to Mike's trailer in Paradise Cove. He offered it for forty dollars a month. I think he felt it was the least he could do after bringing the disruptive Edmundo into our home.

Travels

1967

I settled into the trailer on one of the most beautiful beaches in the world, just steps from my front door. There were tall cliffs tucked into the sandy beach below, keeping traffic noise at bay. There were tidepools to explore and good waves for body surfing. The location lured our friends from the city to come out and visit on weekends. Patsy and Frank, along with a new friend, Patty, had moved to Venice Beach, and Stuart and Ursula and their little girl Michelle joined us at either location alongside the Santa Monica Bay.

My work at Dr. Hodges' office was just right for me. I was becoming acquainted with the families who came in for regular care, and practicing skills for being at the ready if we heard the ambulance coming up the road.

I also began brewing my own plans. My father had always wanted me to go to Denmark as an adult to meet his family. My marriage had prevented that…but maybe this was the opportunity. I wrote to my relatives—my dad was the only one of eight siblings who came to the U.S. so there were plenty of aunts, uncles and cousins to visit, all of whom welcomed me and said I could stay with them as long as I wanted.

And there was my growing friendship with the night-man, Bob. He had been in the Army and then prison, and wasn't yet ready for an ongoing relationship. I was married. A match made in heaven. We kept each other company.

I missed Carl, but I wasn't bored. Indeed, I was starting to find parts of myself that hadn't appeared to me while I was busy with school and working in the hospital. I had never really been on my own, making my own decisions, and it felt good. I found a cheap charter flight to Frankfurt and got up my nerve to tell Dr. Hodges. By the time of my flight I had only been working there for eight months and I didn't want to lose my job. But

I felt this opportunity to explore my Danish roots was important for me and my dad.

Dr. Hodges not only asked a patient, who was a retired nurse to temporarily take my place, he gave me a nice check to help with my travel expenses. Patsy, Frank, Stuart and Ursula saw me off on the charter flight from an oddly dark area of the LAX airport. I was on my way. Patsy gave me a journal to keep track of the journey with a Henry Miller quote: '*Tis only the wondrous traveler that sees a wonder.*

I was determined to be wondrous.

Denmark

I spent five months traveling from one relative to another. They were all very hospitable and kind and took me to all the sights in their particular areas—from the north of Jutland where most of my dad's siblings remained as farmers, to Copenhagen and Odense where some cousins had settled. I gained twenty pounds from their enthusiasm to share Danish pastries, potatoes and sausages, not to mention the aquavit and beer.

Toward the end of the summer, I traveled to Germany where I visited Ursula's family in Bielefeld. They didn't exactly know what to do with me, but found relatives who spoke English. My parents came over and I met them in Frankfurt. My mom and I went to London for a week. We had a good time sightseeing and didn't mention Carl's name once. My dad met us at the boat and we dropped my mom off to stay with the younger generations. In the past, she had spent time on the farm where my father had been born and where his youngest brother now lived. She didn't like it there. No one spoke English and my dad's eldest sister tried to tell her what to do. In Danish.

My dad and I continued to the farm, which may have been the most important part of the journey. I was able to ask him for details about the many family members, especially his generation, who didn't speak English. He seemed so pleased to have me there and show me where he had been an auto-mechanic apprentice in the next town. We hoed the beets together in the early mornings, and I told him about everyone who had been so kind to me.

When I returned to Denmark in 1985 with my sons, all my father's siblings and his stepmother had died. I was so grateful I had been able to meet them all.

Homecoming

In October, I returned to my parents' apartment, to Dr. Hodges' office, the night-man and my friends. I found a guesthouse on Bonsall Drive with one room and a kitchen. I hadn't heard from Carl in quite awhile but within a month, Smokey hollered to me, "It's Carl. He's on the phone." I started crying and shaking. I had tucked away fears that he was dead or just not returning, although I never believed that outcome. He explained he had contracted the measles and was hospitalized. The trip to Easter Island had never materialized, but he had ended up living with an extended family of Easter Islanders in Santiago. There was still hope of the expedition. "Come home," I said. "Okay," he said.

I borrowed money from Frank for Carl's airplane ticket. I met his flight at LAX. He was skinny and haggard-looking but still his handsome self. Tears flowed from both of us. We drove to Patsy and Frank's. More tears. I took him to the guesthouse. I hadn't told my landlords that I had a husband, but they welcomed him.

We had a Christmas gathering there with our friends and my parents and then started talking about where we would live in the new year.

Living on The Knob as Carl's Wife

1968 -1984

First Visit to The Knob

1968

"Hey, I went to the pier this morning to check in with the sport fishing guys," Carl said. "Three of them are living in Decker Canyon, and they told me there is an empty house across from them. Ya wanna take a look?"

"Sure," I replied. We were doing fairly well, reconnecting after almost a year apart, but the small space of my guesthouse did not lend itself to gracious living, even though he had lived with much less in Chile.

We drove up the coast a few days after Christmas and then turned up a canyon road. Each time we had moved since 1965, it seemed we got farther and farther from Santa Monica and my parents. I wondered if, at the age of twenty-four, I was overly attached to them. I had no siblings with whom to discuss this question.

Carl turned onto a dirt driveway at the top of the hill. I looked across a wide valley that was bordered by a long, toothy mountain ridge. I felt surprised that something so grand and rugged was so close to Los Angeles. I later found out it was called Boney Ridge and contained the highest peak in the Santa Monica Mountains, at 3,111 feet. We drove parallel to the ridge for a bit and then angled down and south, passing three other driveways.

The very rutted road ended at a plateau that on first glance looked like a slum, except that it was far from the city.

"Carl, are you kidding me? This looks terrible!"

"Give it a chance," he suggested. "I'll go look for the guys."

The first building we approached was oddly shaped and had plywood sheets nailed over the windows. There was a large pepper tree drooping across the roof and a fading golden bougainvillea attached to one side. Beneath the pepper tree and near the front door was an old house trailer.

Beyond the house—it could not be called a cottage or even a cabin—

were three or four parked cars on the hardened dirt, likely belonging to the fishermen. I assumed they lived in the next visible structure, since I could see glass in the windows instead of plywood. An architect had not been consulted for either the design or the placement of three, almost-square boxes attached to a central open deck. This angular construction was sitting atop cement pilings that were two to three feet high. If it were not filled with weeds and broken-down cardboard boxes, I could have looked under the structures to the canyon beyond.

I groaned.

I slowly emerged from our VW Beetle and started walking around. At the edge of an overgrown lawn near the little house was a row of pine trees. Beyond the trees was a drop-off into thin air. Carl had been home for a bit over a month, and I was one-month pregnant. I believed it would be poor parenting to live in a place where our child could fall off the edge. I couldn't imagine inviting my parents here. They weren't keen on the first four places we had lived. This one was not a step up, and was such a mess that upon my first look around I failed to notice the view of cascading chaparral, the ocean in the distance and several islands marking the horizon.

Carl found me slightly dazed. "The guys told me that a fireman was looking after the property for the owners who live overseas." The fire department, it turned out, was on the other side of the driveway and over a fence—or rather through the fence, since there was a gaping hole in the chain link. At least they would be close and good protection for the wildfires that frequently burned the dry brush on the hillsides.

Pete, the fireman, followed Carl back through the fence to the plateau. He strolled around and finally said, "Yeah, I guess you could rent the place. You could pay fifty bucks a month."

Carl and I looked at each other, silently agreeing that the price was right. I was back at work with Dr. Hodges at $2.75 an hour—my reward for four-and-a-half years of college and RN and B.S. degrees. Carl was welcomed back to the pier where his salary had not improved, but the tips made the income worthwhile. It was not the home of my dreams, but I figured we could move once we reestablished our work lives and saved up some money. We shook hands with Pete and picked a date to move into our temporary dwelling.

THE KNOB

We later found out that the knoll with the four homes was called Barney Knob on the map, no apostrophe on the Barney.

Temporary? I stayed for thirty-two years, seventeen as Carl's wife and fifteen more as his next-door neighbor. Two sons were born while we lived there, and they stayed until they graduated from high school. We added an apostrophe and an 's,' and often referred to living on Barney's Knob, such as: "I'll be back on The Knob at four."

No one knew who Barney was.

Letting in the Light

1968

For the fifth time in as many years, we moved into a new home in January. The sky was clear, but the day was cold. Two of the fishermen helped Carl remove the plywood sheets from the windows. We had entered the house the first day we visited and saw there was furniture, but it was too dark to see what kind. The freestanding wood-burning stove looked like it would be useful.

"What do you think?" Carl asked. It hardly mattered, since we had paid our first month's rent, but I was glad he asked.

"Well, there's more light than I expected." It was the most positive thing I could summon up. I had been able to spruce up our previous dwellings with import-store madras curtains and paper lanterns. I couldn't yet see how to do this here. My guts tightened up as I looked around. The wall next to the front door—the only door—was almost completely glass. The window was not the kind that could be opened, but it let in the light. The wall next to that had a large multi-paned window over a deep sink. I could almost see quaintness, if I squinted.

I counted the walls. There were seven, a heptagon. Against the far wall sat a sofa with an ornate and curvy wooden frame—great potential—but with sagging seats. Between the kitchen sink and the wall by the sofa, brown, pretend-wood panels had been erected to create a bedroom, in which stood a cherry wood, four-poster double bed. The panels did not reach the ceiling. There was no ceiling, just the inside of the roof, which was multi-angled to accommodate the seven walls. Tucked in a corner was an enclosed toilet and sink. Next to that, a freestanding metal shower with a grungy, plastic curtain. I could not envision this place in *Better Homes & Gardens* anytime soon. Or even *Family Circle*, but I was relieved that we had indoor plumbing.

"Welcome home!" Carl said. We both laughed, not a chuckle or guffaw, but more like a gusher of sound that indicated, "Now what do we do?"

I continued working at Dr. Hodges' and "decorating" on my days off. I painted the kitchen area bright white with royal blue trim to match the Danish dishes I had collected from relatives on my recent trip to Denmark. I checked out an upholstery book from the library and bought some blue-green woven material to redo the sofa from Lincoln Fabrics near Venice Beach. When I considered it done, it looked pretty good, but the seats still drooped. No matter how hard I tugged on the canvas straps to hold the cushions, it wasn't hard enough. We sat on it anyway.

My belly was growing. I made monthly visits to the obstetrician's office in Westwood Village, where the streets were aglow with purple jacaranda blossoms. Carl created an oddly angled "nursery" by erecting more brown panels. I covered the walls with very bright yellow-print wallpaper, and Ursula passed on her daughter's crib and changing table. They fit, with just enough room for us to squeeze in and out.

We were starting to feel at home. As the winter moved into spring we watched the thick grass grow greener. I planted zinnia seeds in a little patch outside the front door, between the house and the trailer.

I had hopes of beauty, despite the forlorn plateau.

Carole

1968

My first full summer working for Dr. Hodges was traumatic. There were fatal traffic accidents, which were not a frequent occurrence. A two year old boy drowned in the family pool. A husky young man died from hitting his head on a rock after slipping down a cliff in Malibu Canyon.

At the same time, our baby was growing. I had felt the quickening one day while lying on the blue sofa. The first flutter was almost indiscernible, but I stayed still and waited. It came again, and then again. The baby was now a real person to me and I couldn't wait for each new development.

Carole, Carl's sister, called one day. She had moved to Oregon, following her mother and step-dad, but was not happy there.

"I am feeling restless up here. Can I come and visit?"

"Of course!" We hadn't seen her in months and looked forward to spending time with her. She adored her brother, and he adored her. Carole and I had become good friends. I had introduced her to Anne of Green Gables, and she thanked me by making an oil painting of Anne and her friends in a forest. She was about to turn nineteen and wanted to celebrate with us in California.

Virginia, Carl's mother called. "I'm trying to convince Carole to take the Greyhound down. She wants to hitchhike!" she said in dismay. "She's finally agreed to take the bus, but I don't know what has gotten into her."

Carole reported later, "I got off the bus in Crescent City. I just wanted to feel free and have some adventure!"

While she told us that she had one scary ride, from which she escaped in one piece, she was exhilarated by the experience. The final ride dropped her at the corner of Pacific Coast Highway, or PCH, as it is known. She hiked up the road to my office and we hugged. I made arrangements to drive her home on my lunch hour.

On the way, I pointed out some of the places where the big accidents had occurred.

"Why are you telling me this?" she asked.

"I don't know. I guess it's just been a little freaky here lately. I'm sorry, that is kind of gross."

We passed a semi-truck turned on its side at the bottom of PCH by Zuma Beach. The atmosphere was unusually tense.

Carl had been hired to captain a large schooner called *The Swift*, from Costa Rica to Los Angeles. He got home and we had a week of fun days with Carole, hiking in the hills around our new home. We cooked artichokes, which we three considered to be the best possible vehicle for melted butter.

She came to the Hollywood Bowl with me and my parents. We had the usual picnic in one of the pocket parks, the way my little family had done all my life. Then we listened to music by Gershwin under the stars.

On the weekend, she hitchhiked to Santa Barbara and visited our friend, Steve. She arrived back at our house, safe and sound, saying she had had a great time.

When I woke up on Monday morning, I found Karen, Carole's stepsister, and Karen's boyfriend Bob, camping on the lawn. We had breakfast together and discussed the merits of hitchhiking, or lack thereof. I left for work. It was a beautiful, sunny summer morning.

A few hours into our workday, we got a call from the ambulance driver.

"We're thirty minutes out. It looks serious. Three people in a car crash."

Smokey and I did what we always did with such a call: we propped open the back doors, laid out the blood pressure cuffs and stethoscopes and continued with our regular patients until we heard the siren and could see the ambulance coming up the road.

When the ambulance backed up to the doors of the emergency room, I saw Bob get out of the front passenger seat. I smiled, confused, but relieved that he seemed to be okay. Then I realized Karen must be in the back of the ambulance.

The ambulance guys, Frank and Pete, wheeled a gurney into our ER room. Karen was wailing and wailing. I had read about such a sound coming from a person with a concussion, but had never heard it before. She was unconscious. I grabbed a cuff and started taking her blood pressure. Her pulse was rapid but within normal limits. Her elbow looked wrong and she was bleeding over her right eye. I remembered she wore contact lenses. I took them out and taped them into an envelope.

Dr. Hodges was off for the afternoon, but fortunately Dr. Smith was on-call and was a good doctor, not always the case with the on-call docs needing to earn extra cash.

Smokey was tending to Bob in one of the exam rooms, when another gurney was pushed into the ER.

"Oh my God," I screamed. "It's Carole! It's Carl's sister! What's she doing here?" I was confused, until I realized that Bob must have offered to drive her back up to Santa Barbara.

Carole looked okay—that is, there was no blood. But she was very quiet and not moving.

Dr. Smith moved over to her gurney after making sure the IV was working properly with Karen, who was still wailing.

"Carole's okay, isn't she?" I asked Dr. Smith. I knew something was wrong. I had felt her pulse and it was thready and weak. I was struggling with the blood pressure cuff due to my own nervousness. I think my busy actions were an attempt to cover up my fear.

Dr. Smith took my hands from her arm and pulled me next to him.

"Look. I want you to see this. Both her pupils are completely dilated. Her prognosis is not good."

I looked at him and looked at Carole's eyes, but also looked at Carole. She seemed so peaceful and comfortable. I started shouting, "Well, do something!"

"Tell me where the intubation tube is kept," Dr. Smith said clearly and firmly.

"I don't know," I cried. "Dr. Hodges always does a tracheotomy for something like this."

By now Dr. Hodges' wife had arrived. She was also a nurse. She and the secretary pulled me away from the scene and took me into the doctor's office. They later said they were concerned about my being in the midst of this stress when I was in my eighth month of pregnancy.

I heard the back doors open and heard Dr. Hodges' voice. I barged out of the office, sobbing and yelling, "Do something, Dr. Hodges!" At the same time, I saw Pete and Frank carrying Carole's gurney into Room Three, where we put patients who had died.

"Oh no, no!" I went back into the doctor's office and curled up on the floor, over my big belly. Despite my anguish, I realized I had knocked my nurse's cap off and it was now pinned onto the side of my head, with my hair falling down. I was aware that it was very weird to notice this silly thing while Carole was dead in Room Three, and I cried even harder.

I didn't go into that room.

And I never saw her again.

The Aftermath

1968

Carl was in town doing errands and visiting our friend, Patty. Dr. Hodges called him there and told him about Carole. Patty drove him to the office because he was too upset to drive. By the time I saw him, he was pale with the green tinge I came to learn accompanied his pallor when he was scared. He loved his little sister. He wasn't crying. It seemed like he was numb and blanking out the news. He didn't enter Room Three either. We hugged, but he wasn't talking. We stood around for a bit, not knowing what to do. I finally drove us home, and we lay down on the four-poster bed and soon went to sleep.

Dr. Hodges had also called Carl's mother and told her husband what had happened. He got her to her doctor who prescribed sedatives. They made plans to fly down. I don't remember who told Carole's father, Eric, but he made arrangements for the funeral at Forest Lawn and reported that he had chosen a burial plot with a good view. I wondered who the view was for, but was glad he was helping with the details.

Virginia told me we needed to offer food for family and friends after the funeral. I hadn't thought of that. I realized I knew nothing about the protocol following a death. My grandmother had died when I was fifteen, and I recalled going to her funeral in a church, but I didn't recall food or socializing.

A day later, I drove into Santa Monica and parked near the hospital. I found Karen's room number. She was awake, but groggy. I sat next to her bed.

"Hi," she said as she focused on my face. "My eye hurts and I can't bend my elbow."

I could see bandages over her eye and she had a cast on her right arm.

"How's the food here?" I asked.

"Crummy, but I'm not hungry."

We tried a few more banal topics but neither of us mentioned the accident or that Carole was dead. I knew this was an opportunity I was missing, to be honest and close to Karen. Again, I realized I was unprepared for death or what happens to the survivors after a loved one's death. I grew more anxious by the moment and prepared to leave. I told her I would return.

I didn't.

While I was at the hospital, I went up one floor to visit one of our family practice patients. She was in her late thirties with two teenage sons and had terminal cancer. I had been her office nurse during the year of her diagnosis and treatment and had grown fond of her and her family. Now it looked like she was not going to get well.

"Hi, Bev," I greeted her.

She smiled and welcomed me into her room.

"How are you feeling?" I asked.

"Oh, not great. You can see how thin I look, but I weigh more because the malignancy is growing. Weird, huh?"

"I weigh more too because the baby is growing," I responded, about as stupidly as I can imagine.

What was I thinking? There I was with another opportunity to listen to her concerns and fears, but I didn't know how. How had I made it through nursing school without learning how to provide emotional comfort to a patient and a family member?

I drove to the nearby Safeway in a daze. I tossed a canned ham into my basket and paper plates and cups. I am sure I picked out salad fixings and some cookies, but I can't remember past the ham. When I got to the checkout stand, the man said, "Ma'am, I can't accept your check. It's not from Santa Monica."

"What?" I shrieked. "I live in the next town, not Nebraska!"

"Sorry," he said, looking at me with raised eyebrows.

I found a phone booth in the parking lot and called my mom, who up to that point I had not even told about Carole's death. She lived a few blocks from the market and came over right away. I was sitting on a cement post crying when she arrived. She held me until I calmed down and was able to tell her what had happened. I apologized for not telling her sooner.

"Okay, let's go pay for your groceries."

We walked back into the store and could not find the cart of food I had left.

"Sir," I called to the checker. "Where's my cart?"

"We put the food away. I didn't know you were coming back."

I started crying again. This situation, so minor compared to what was really happening in my life, seemed unsolvable.

My mom calmed me down, something that was not a usual occurrence in our lives, and together we refilled the basket. My mom wrote her Santa Monica check, and somehow I drove the thirty-five miles home.

Virginia and her husband Don arrived. She insisted on going to the mortuary to see Carole, which at the time I thought was morbid and strange. I didn't realize that Virginia had already experienced enough deaths to know that this viewing provided comfort and allowed her to quietly be with her daughter and say good-bye. Neither Carl nor I went with her.

The next day, Carl and I drove across the city to Forest Lawn in Glendale for the funeral. Carl asked me to stop several times to buy canned martinis. I had never seen him drink a martini, let alone a cocktail out of a can. It appeared to be the quickest way for him to forget what was actually happening. I just drove and wept.

The funeral was in a beautiful chapel, but was as generic as could be. The pastor didn't know Carole and had to give his talk based on some notes her parents had provided. Nothing about it was comforting.

It was clear that Virginia was also under the influence—she seemed to giggle about odd little things, in the midst of her tears. She also reported how beautiful Carole had looked in the viewing room.

It got worse. Virginia invited the friends who attended the funeral to come back to our house for food. The wounds from the divorce of Carl's parents had still not healed, so even though they were both present at the funeral itself, we couldn't ask his dad and Alice to come back to our house for the lunch.

I drove a subdued Carl home from Forest Lawn as fast as I could, so I could set out the paper plates and ham.

Should I slice it? Should I cut up the fruit?

Hour by hour I was learning how little I knew about anything from food to dying. I don't recall what Carl was doing as the guests arrived.

About a dozen people squeezed into our little house. Despite my attempts at upholstery, lawn mowing and zinnia-tending, it was still a mountain shack, and this was still a funeral lunch for a nineteen-year-old girl.

Virginia's normal nervous giggle was now at high pitch, I assumed from the tranquilizers, as well as trying to be gracious when she had just lost her daughter. Even though it was a beautiful summer day, we had no yard furniture to sit on outdoors. It was a dismal scene I would relive for years to come.

The guests finally left, and Carl and I climbed onto the bed. We did not talk about Carole or death or what any of it meant to us. We slept into the next day again, as we did on the day of her death.

The next afternoon, I lay down on the grass and started thinking about life and the end of life. I saw that the raw emotions surrounding the accident and the sorrow were incredibly difficult for most people to discuss, including me. I was so sad that Carole's parents could not embrace each other, even at this tragic moment. I made a pledge to myself that if I ever got divorced, I would make sure both Carl and I could comfortably attend weddings or funerals for people we both loved, together. And that I would also learn more about dying and death.

We now had to begin focusing on the impending birth of our first child, only weeks away.

John Erik

1968

Virginia and Don returned to Oregon. The trash men took the used paper plates and cups away. I mowed the lawn and admired the zinnias, which were now in full bloom—brilliant red, purple, orange and yellow. I needed something bright after the preceding weeks.

About a week later, I called Dr. Hodges and said I wanted to come back to the office. Carl had gone to work, and I felt awkward and lonely during the long sad days.

"Come on in," he said, and I did.

A few weeks after Carole's death and funeral, I took a work-break to go to the bathroom. Something felt different when I peed. I looked into the toilet and something looked different there, too.

I stuck my head out the bathroom door.

"Smokey! Can you come here?"

"What's up?"

"Do you mind taking a look in the toilet?" One thing about being a nurse, it's easy to discuss most anything.

"It's the pink show!" she shouted.

"I thought so," I said. "I've read about it but never seen it in person." By the time soon-to-be mothers arrived during my OB rotation, their pink shows had been flushed away.

Smokey and I looked at each other, grinning.

"Oh my God, this is it!" I realized. The waiting was almost over.

"Let's order a pizza to celebrate," Smokey suggested. She did that while I called Carl to tell him the delivery was imminent. I already had my hospital bag packed, since this was the week of the actual due date.

After lunch and the afternoon patients were seen, I drove to the Knob. Carl had gone to the store and bought the makings for Tin Roofs—

vanilla ice cream, Spanish peanuts, the kind with the red skins flaking off, and chocolate fudge sauce. I don't recall where he learned this particular concoction, or what it had to do with impending childbirth, but we both were feeling celebratory and nervous. The OB doc said to stay at home as long as possible, since it was my first child.

After gorging on the Tin Roofs, we climbed onto the cherry-wood four-poster and turned out the light.

"You awake?"

"Yeah."

"I can't sleep."

"Me, neither."

Suddenly, we both heard a loud and unfamiliar sound, kind of like *thonk,* if it were in a comic book.

"What the heck?"

"I don't know!"

But then we were both feeling damp, and we did know. My water had broken with a flourish.

I called the doctor again.

"You might as well come in since you live so far from town."

It was almost midnight. As we drove down PCH, a large moon kept peeking over the cliffs as we rounded the curves in the road. I was beginning to feel some very mild contractions. In less than a month, I was on my way to Santa Monica Hospital again. While I was happy about this momentous event, it was difficult not to connect it with my last trip there.

We were standing at the reception desk filling out forms when Carl gently elbowed my arm.

"I don't think holding your knees together is doing the trick." He pointed to the floor. More liquid was pouring from me and creating a puddle around my feet. I was taken to the labor and delivery area in a wheelchair.

I found out later that Lamaze classes had been available in 1968, but neither my doctor nor I had heard of them. But I knew I wanted to try natural childbirth and asked him about it during the pregnancy.

"We'll see what we can do," he said. "Read this book, *The ABC's of Natural Childbirth*, and we'll talk about it later." The book was helpful but it was a lonely process without the classes I attended with my second child.

The labor room was partitioned into half a dozen spaces with curtains. Every time an expectant mother was wheeled in or out, Carl was asked to leave our cubicle. The seven or eight hours that passed were frequently interrupted. A nurse gave me a shot of Demerol when my contractions became strong, without asking me.

The delivery itself went well, except I was so sleepy from the injection that I could barely stay awake to hold our new son, John Erik—named after the two grandfathers.

Carl was at our side in the recovery room, but he had not been allowed in the delivery room.

"I was so nervous the whole time I was in the waiting room. So were the other dads. No one would tell us anything," he said later.

His green tinge was fading by the time he was able to hold the baby and see that we were both alive and well. I am sure that his teenage experience of having a baby die had increased his anxiety in the waiting room.

I stayed one night at the hospital. The next day as Carl drove John Erik and me home, we stopped at the doctor's office to show off the baby. I loved the *oohs* and *aahs* from the office staff and some of the patients who were there.

Carl had started ferrying workers to the oil rigs in the Santa Barbara Channel, working a week on and a week off. The baby and I stayed at my mom's every other weekend and it was a joy to watch her bond with him. I don't think I ever felt the intense love from her that I saw her giving to our baby. Maybe it was some kind of mother-daughter stuff, but I was pleased to see her happy.

I hoped that the deaths of Martin Luther King, Jr., Bobby Kennedy and Carole were going to end the streak of shocking losses in the momentous year of 1968. I felt that our baby's birth shifted that trajectory. The rest of the year included learning how to be parents, watching the baby grow and change each week, and continuing to make our home more beautiful and livable.

Rain

1969

That winter we had the most rain ever. Well, maybe it wasn't the most rain ever, but it felt that way, living in an almost one-room house, a long dirt driveway that was often impassable for our cars and cloth diapers strung across the width of the "great room." It wasn't great. We felt trapped.

At least our son John Erik was sleeping through the night and was mellow and sweet when he was awake.

Carl was home most of every other week. I had resigned from Dr. Hodges with the baby's birth, so the three of us were cabin-bound. No television, no newspaper delivery in the canyon. We didn't play cards or even Scrabble in those days. Our closest friends lived thirty miles away. There was no point in cleaning the little house…more wet footprints obliterated any attempts.

Yet, in some ways it was a blessing in disguise, if a very damp disguise. From the time we met, we had both been going to school, or working, or off on our separate travels. We hadn't taken any vacations together.

We took turns caring for and playing with Erik. When he slept, we read, and we talked. There was time to continue exploring our relationship and sharing our histories, short as they still were.

"So, what do you think happens to your soul after you die?" I asked one day. We had not talked about Carole's death since the settling of the external events surrounding those difficult days.

"What do you think the soul is?" he responded.

"It's what remains after we die. You know, who we really are."

"How do you know that?"

"I just know." In fact, I didn't know how I knew that, but I did. My picture had nothing to do with the Father, Son and Holy Ghost of my Presbyterian experience, but it had somehow developed in my psyche.

"Where is it?" Carl asked.

"Inside us. It fills all the spaces that don't have organs or blood vessels. Then when we die, it leaves. Maybe it goes out through our nose or mouth. Or ears. I've never seen it happen, so I am not sure about that part of it."

"Who told you that?" Carl asked, raising his eyebrows.

"No one. I just know it. What do you think?"

"I've never thought much about it. Maybe that's why I don't want to talk about Carole. I just see her as gone."

At the time of Carole's death, I had been reading *The Philosopher's Stone* by Johannes Anker Larsen. My mother had recommended it, telling me she had read books about Denmark to understand my dad better. A young woman in the story who was also nineteen died of a mysterious ailment. She was not fearful, even when she knew she was dying. Either the young woman herself, or one of her family members said some version of, "Sometimes, a soul is born just to bring light to others. Then they don't need to live a long life."

This was very impactful to me—and maybe contributed somewhat to my ideas about the soul. I copied it and sent it to Virginia. She later told me it helped her grieve more than anything else that came her way after her daughter's death.

I understood why Carl's sister's death was so difficult for him. He just shut down. I think I carried Carole's life story for him.

The Screen Porch

1969

Our tiny house expanded during the second summer. Carl extended the back wall of the living room into a screened-in porch. It was spacious, light and airy. Grass matting and paper lanterns from Pier 1 made the room feel tropical.

We put a double bed in one end of the new room. Sleeping almost outside was divine. The sounds of crickets and frogs—even though there was no water nearby that we knew of—lulled us to sleep. The symphony of morning birdcalls was so cheering that we didn't mind waking at dawn.

On the other end of the rectangular room was a low round table made from a cable spool—a common solution for cheap furniture in those days. It was gussied up with sanding and varnish. We sat on pillows around the table. John Erik was walking by this time and tall enough to lean his elbows on the low table so he could chat with us using his developing vocabulary. Patsy and Frank came out on weekends and after cooling off in the Doughboy pool we had installed at the end of the lawn, we gathered around the table sipping tequila shooters and eating guacamole and chips.

We excitedly invited my parents out to see our new room. They weren't keen about sitting on the floor but were polite and complimentary. It was so much prettier than our living room, they may have meant the compliments. Even though I was now in my later twenties, I still craved my mother's approval. My dad always gave his.

Carl's job of ferrying the workers out to the oil rigs off Santa Barbara came to an end. To fill in for the financial loss, I signed up with a nursing registry. I was called two to three times a week to drive into either Santa Monica Hospital or St. John's Hospital. This work was torture for me. From the time I woke up in the morning, I was anxious.

Would I be called, or not? Should I get dirty in the garden or wait until past the call hour?

Once there, it was worse. Each hospital and each floor was different and unfamiliar. This did not suit my stolid nature of needing to know and be comfortable with my surroundings and procedures.

One night a resident doctor came into the curtained area where I was sitting with an elderly, unconscious patient.

"I'm here to do a spinal tap," he announced. "Please roll her onto her side."

The patient had had a stroke and was dead weight. I recalled my instructions to maintain an open airway when turning an unconscious patient over. I slid pillows under her head and held onto her side and back, steadying her while the doctor inserted a very large needle into her low back.

He held the syringe up when he finished. "Look," he nodded his head toward the syringe. "It's all blood. She's a goner."

"Oh," I might have uttered, as he walked out of the curtained cubicle without further word.

I was still holding onto the patient and I let her gently down onto her back. The area was very quiet and somehow intense. I couldn't hear my own breathing, and then I noticed I couldn't hear hers either—she wasn't breathing.

Oh my God. Did I not place the pillows properly? Was it my fault? Did I kill her?

I had met her family earlier in the evening.

Would I have to tell them, "Oh by the way, I just rolled your mother over and she seems to be dead?"

I ran to the nurse's station. The resident was there, writing notes.

"Doctor, can you come with me? Mrs. Brown is not breathing," I said shakily.

He followed me back to the cubicle and said something like, "OK, I'll go write it up." I really don't know what he said but he definitely wasn't concerned with her or me. I was spared telling the family by the intervention of the charge nurse.

I was three years out of nursing school, but between my five-month hiatus in Denmark and the fact that my nursing school dean believed in teaching good judgment techniques rather than three years of full-time clinical duty, I was not prepared for the technical aspects of nursing. Our training about dying and death was also meager.

    I couldn't wait to drive the thirty miles home. I recall hearing "Bridge Over Troubled Water" on the radio as I crossed the Malibu Lagoon. I was glad for the bridge concept and was eagerly hoping to sleep the rest of the night and wake up to the birdsongs in our new screen porch.

Ruthann

1970

Mike from the dive shop had brought his new girlfriend, Jill, to meet me when I lived in his trailer. We became friends, although there was always a bit of tension between Carl and Jill. She had a sharp edge but was funny and smart. A couple of years later, we received an elegant wedding invitation, as well as additional invites to wedding activities.

At a pre-wedding luncheon at Madame Wu's on Wilshire Boulevard, I met Ruthann.

"Well, how are ya'?" the cute lady said when we were introduced. Her New York accent was strong and didn't fit her. She looked more as if she'd come from Minnesota than New York. She was tiny, at least compared to me. Her features were delicate except for enormous eyes that were neither green nor blue, but not quite turquoise. She had thick blond hair. I could tell it would always do what she wanted it to do. Mine rarely did.

Ruthann and Jill had been teaching together at a private school in Brentwood, and I had been hearing about her from Jill. Ruthann and I chatted, covering some of the basic personal facts, me a nurse, she a teacher, me with one child, she with none...yet. She had an enthusiastic way of speaking, and I looked forward to seeing her again.

A week later, the rehearsal dinner took place on the top floor of a Santa Monica hotel with a great view. It happened that Carl and I were seated at the same table as Ruthann and her husband, Michael. Carl and Michael seemed comfortable chatting as well. I had found it was not often that husbands of friends also liked each other.

The wedding itself was held at the home of the bride's brother in Topanga Canyon. The Spanish hacienda-style house had a balcony from which we heard and could see a flautist and violinist playing Vivaldi and later, Pachelbel's *Canon*. Ancient oak trees shaded the courtyard. Servers milled through the crowds of guests with trays of hors d'oeuvres and flutes of champagne while we waited for the ceremony to begin. We found Michael and Ruthann and continued exchanging stories.

Ruthann had graduated from Tufts University, a school I had only known from novels. Michael was a tall, slender attorney with a snappy sense of humor. We sat together again during the exchange of vows and the buffet dinner that followed.

Ruthann had an engaging way about her. She nudged me with an elbow and with direct eye contact asked, "So how long have you guys been married?"

"Almost five years," I replied, "If we don't count the sabbatical."

"Ooh, tell me about that!" she said, without skipping a beat. I did.

"And you?"

"Almost four. Michael's a bit jealous, which is why we moved west. He didn't like that my ex-boyfriend lived near."

"Carl too! Except that I don't have an ex-boyfriend…well, there is an ex-lover, who hardly counts in my book. But Carl sure didn't want to hear about that chapter…even though he asked."

Ruthann laughed. Her eyes seemed even bigger because she had applied some sparkling eye make-up to go with the brocade dress she was wearing. "I wore this to our second wedding we had for Michael's parents' benefit. We eloped for the first one," she told me. "I never thought I'd wear it again."

I was wearing a cotton dress I had made. The pattern looked better than the dress did. We both had our hair in upsweeps.

By the time it was over, we had exchanged phone numbers and made plans to meet for dinner. We seemed an unlikely match for friends—east and west, Jewish lawyer and hippie-looking artist, rich and poor.

A few weeks later we drove into Santa Monica and had dinner at their apartment on San Vicente. John Erik was with us, and we could see by the end of the evening they were drawn to him as well.

We stood outside their front door after dinner, talking. We were watching John Erik who was squatting at the edge of the pool chatting with an older man who was in the water. John Erik had his elbow across his bent knee and was holding forth as if he were fifty.

"Well, I am four years old and those are my parents standing over there."

He glanced over his shoulder as if to let us know he was aware of us. He was not quite two but already had the élan and vocabulary of a grown-up. He had certainly won the hearts of Michael and Ruthann who were grinning and hanging on his every word, which might have continued into the night had we not interrupted.

If our wedding visits hadn't cemented our friendship, their connection with our little boy certainly did. We often joked that the Saphiers sought our company because they liked John Erik. But there it was. And it continued for over forty years.

Fire

1970

I was working at Dr. Hodges' office one cool, foggy September morning. The phone rang. It was Smokey, who was off for the day. She lived about halfway up Malibu Canyon.

"There's a fire in Calabasas and it looks like it's moving through the canyon quickly. You guys better get out of there right now!"

The secretaries and I stood in the doctor's office doorway telling him the news. He had his feet up on his desk in a rare quiet moment. "No way," he said. "That's fifteen or twenty miles from here."

"But Smokey said it's traveling this way. Fast!"

I looked out the window and up the hill leading to Malibu Canyon by the Rand Corporation and Presbyterian Church.

"Oh my God," I screamed. "I see flames. Right there! Look!"

The doctor's feet came off the desk and he swiveled in the office chair. He leapt up.

"Okay, grab what you can. The patients' files will be safe in the metal cabinets."

Margaret took the basket containing files for that day's patients. Gert grabbed her bookkeeping journals, and they left.

I knocked on the door of the new night-man, Harold's apartment. I knew he had gone into town, and his new French wife, Genevieve, was there alone.

"Genevieve, come with me. We have to leave."

By now the electricity was off and the sky was dark with smoke. The Santa Ana winds were driving the fire at lightning speed.

"My glasses," she wailed. "I can't see a thing."

We scrambled around for a bit but couldn't find them. I took her hand and pulled her toward the back door.

We got into my car. It wouldn't start. Dead battery! I forgot to turn off the lights from driving in the morning fog.

Just as we got out of the car a couple, Richard and Donna, who were patients, drove up to see if they could help.

"Get in," Richard said. He did a screeching U-turn and we started down the road. By now the plant nursery next door was on fire and we tore through vivid flames for a few moments.

"Let's go over to the Mayfair Market so we can see what's going on," Richard suggested. It was on the other side of PCH and seemed safe enough. There, we found Dr. Hodges, Gert and Margaret.

We paced around looking up the road, although we couldn't see the office clearly due to the smoke. Suddenly, there was a loud boom and a fireball shooting up into the sky, above the smoke.

Dr. Hodges said, "I bet it was the oxygen tanks exploding." So much for my car, I thought, which I had left parked outside the office.

I asked Richard if he would drive Genevieve and me to Venice, where she said Harold was. I knew we could hang out at Patsy and Frank's and make contact with family and friends with their phone.

I called Carl and told him to pack up John Erik and Coco and everything he could fit into our car and come to Venice by way of the Valley, because at the rate the fire was moving I believed it would be up there in no time.

We found Harold, and Genevieve went with him. Carl arrived with John Erik, our dog and the car full of our belongings. We sat with Patsy and Frank for awhile, telling them what had happened. I remembered we had a key to my parents' apartment in Santa Monica; they were camping in Europe. We parked in their garage. Despite everything, we slept long and deep.

When we got up the next morning, we found that someone had broken into our old Land Rover. We could see Carl's guitar and my sewing machine were missing, but he couldn't remember what else he had packed. We called the police and they came by and took a report. Within an hour, they called back to say one of them had spotted a "hippie-type guy," staggering up Pico Boulevard, lugging a sewing machine and guitar. The other belongings were in a bag, all of which were returned to me.

The next day we drove to Malibu, following the blackened road to the charred and collapsed remains of the office. There my car sat, dusted with ash, but otherwise it looked normal. It turned out that Frank and Pete came after we left to see if they could help. They had pushed my car away from the building, saving it.

Genevieve and Harold were there too, poking around. They had lost everything, since the night-man's apartment was their residence at the time. Nothing remained of the office except the chimney. No file cabinets, no metal X-ray machine and definitely no metal oxygen tanks.

For months, we shared space at a nearby doctor's office. Then Dr. Hodges had a large trailer placed on the same spot, not as charming as the white frame house with its tangerine trees growing outside the examination room windows. It was to be temporary, but he practiced there until he retired, many years later.

The fire never made it to Barney's Knob…that time.

Baubles & Bangles

1971

I love things that sparkle and shine. As a child, I indulged that passion, especially on Halloween—as a princess, or ballerina—not so much wearing a witch costume.

But it wasn't until I was in my thirties that I was able to embrace the passion to full measure. Patsy and I signed up for Belly Dance classes at Everywoman's Village in Van Nuys. It was a bit of a schlep, but we had watched Diane Webber and her "Perfumes of Araby" dance troupe at the Renaissance Faire. We hoped to become good enough to join the troupe one day. That never happened.

Meanwhile, as we mastered the finger cymbals and the art of circling the rib cage in one direction and the pelvis in the other, we were encouraged to make costumes. I could hardly wait.

Our first stop was Frederick's of Hollywood, the shop that advertised thong undies and bras with holes cut out for the nipples to show. Our goal was a low-cut bra with pockets in which to insert push-up pads, to achieve cleavage—when there wasn't much to cleave. I managed to get two sets of pads into my bra with satisfying results.

Then came the artful stitching of silky fabric onto the bra and sequins along the contour lines of the bra and the straps.

There followed more swirling shawls to decorate and long skirts or billowing pantaloons—sequins, crystals on strings and rhinestones galore. My costume was gorgeous.

The big accomplishment was the hip girdle—an item with so many dangling coins that it could be heard blocks away while shimmying.

Possibly because of the allure of the push-up bra and my new cleavage, I had become pregnant with my second child. I had to devote my decorative aspirations to a caftan with a hip scarf that would not constrain my baby. I watched with envy as Patsy fashioned her girdle.

Patsy and I continued with the classes and performed at bar mitzvahs and lamb roast parties for whomever invited us. We only asked that the audience drank enough wine to dull their critical senses before we slithered onto the makeshift stages, finger cymbals clanging and beads sparkling.

Neighbors
1971 – 1973

PHINE

A few years passed. Pete Garcia, the fireman overseeing our part of the Knob, deemed Carl and me to be responsible enough to take over his job.

A woman named Josephine—Erik called her "Phine"—had moved into the collection of modular boxes with her twelve-year-old son. The good news was that she worked for the nearby probation camps, and they gave her seedlings that were used by the work crews to reforest the hillsides after fires.

Phine was assiduous in planting them everywhere—mostly pines, but also a mimosa tree. She carried buckets of water to each plant every weekend. We could see them growing.

The less good news was that she was anxious and sharp of tongue, and her son was left on his own during the hours between school letting out and when she got home from work. We asked him not to swim in our Doughboy Pool when no one was home. We asked Josephine to tell him not to do so. We took the ladder out whenever we were both gone, but to no avail.

We felt responsible for his safety and our liability. After more warnings, we told her she had to move.

A few days later, there was a loud rapping at our front door. I opened it and there stood Phine, spitting mad. Her long white hair had mostly escaped its ponytail. Her eyes were glaring at me, and her jaw was clenched. She finally managed to speak.

"I just want you to know that I've put your names on my Catholic Prayer list. I asked them to pray for your deaths!" She spit out each word.

"What?" I gasped.

"You heard me," she said, stamping her right foot.

"Do Catholics really do that?" I asked.

"Of course they do. How else do we get rid of evil people?"

That's kind of nutty.

But I said, "I'm sorry you're angry at us, but we asked you kindly for several months to tell John to stay out of the pool every day when no one was watching out for him."

She turned and stomped across the lawn to her house without another word.

Pola

Erik woke up from a nap.

"Let's walk up and get the mail," I said as I hugged him out of his crib. We all enjoyed the half-mile trek up the driveway with the view of the Boney Ridge once we rounded the first house above us.

There were relatively new neighbors in that house. When I had asked their names, they responded "Pola and Raj." They both had slight though different accents so I decided they must have meant Paula and Roger.

They *were* Pola and Raj. She was from Germany and had been named after the actress Pola Negri. Raj was actually Ronald from New Jersey but had added flourish by changing it to Rajem. Raj for short.

Pola joined Erik and me on our walk to the mailboxes. I decided to regale her with the hilarious claim made by Phine.

When I finished my story, Pola put her hand on my arm and said, "Oh my dear, you must surround yourself with white light!"

That sounded just as nutty as Phine's proclamation!

"Really? What's white light and how do you do that?"

She looked perplexed as if my not knowing about surrounding oneself with white light was very odd.

I know we were barely out of the 1960s, but aside from having long hair and wearing long skirts…and being married to an artist with a long red beard…we were not hippies. I had yet to delve into the spiritual aspects of that decade. Pola was the first to enlighten me.

Phine and John moved away. The tree seedlings grew over the decades, except for the ones we had to cut down because they had been planted too close to the house and threatened to push out window panes.

We slowly began taking over the modular boxes ourselves.

We began spending more time with Pola. She offered to show me how to make gold-wire jewelry. She lived in a cottage behind the main house, where Raj and their two sons, Christo and Jeno, lived. This was an unusual arrangement and a portent of my own future, but I didn't know that yet.

In the hours when Erik was napping, I often sat at Pola's thick wooden desk, bending the square gold wire with jeweler's pliers. It was quiet and satisfying work, even though I wasn't particularly creative at my attempts. I followed her designs as I practiced. We chatted in between instructions, and my moaning *Darn it!* when I made a mistake.

Pola said things like "Well, in my last life, I was a courtesan in Europe," or "Rajem and I are together again because we didn't work out our issues in our last lives together," and "Christo and Jeno came in to help us." In the early months, I thought this was kinda crazy. I had heard of reincarnation but never gave it much thought, filing it alongside something that I had read that stated that East Indians would rather starve than eat the cows that roamed their streets. But as time passed, it started to make some sense.

"How do you know all this stuff?" I asked.

"Oh my dear," she responded. "I just know. I can remember some of my past lives. Sometimes, experiences I have or people I meet, remind me of other times."

"Is there something I can read to learn about it?"

"Read about Theosophy," she suggested. I remembered that word from the Danish book I read around the time Carole died, but I had not absorbed the concepts behind it.

I didn't read anything for a long time but my mind started opening bit by bit to different ways of thinking about life and death. My Presbyterian upbringing had not included much that was helpful for figuring out what life was all about.

Another new experience that Pola and Raj exposed us to was food. They were vegetarians before it became fashionable. We first learned this when Christo and Jeno would stand at our front door on Sunday mornings, practically drooling as we fried bacon. When we invited them to join us they said, "Oh no, we can't eat meat."

Neither Carl nor I had ever considered this possibility. What, no bacon? Steaks? Chicken? No BBQs?

"Does being a vegetarian mean not eating fish either?" I asked Pola, thinking of all the seafood Carl brought home from scuba diving.

"Of course. We don't eat any flesh," she said. I had never considered fish as being flesh exactly. It knocked down the desirability factor a bit.

Another food moment was when I helped carry in a bag of groceries to their kitchen. I started to set it on the counter when Raj grabbed it from me, shouting, "No! Not there. That's where we prepare food. The bag is dirty!"

I looked at the bag.

It didn't look dirty to me, just a regular brown paper bag. But then it was his kitchen.

Raj had a large scar and indentation under his jaw. Pola told me he had had cancer and recovered by eating organic food and no meat.

Raj and Pola stayed a couple of years. The clothes that passed from Christo to Jeno as they grew, soon fit Erik, and we were happy to receive them. The boys were kind playmates for Erik as he moved into toddlerhood.

But life on the Knob became complicated when Pola fell in love with an artist named Richard. He painted intricate scenes on the back of glass, which meant he painted the foreground first and followed that with the middle and backgrounds. This talent led to exquisite scenes of mythical creatures and castles, trees and flowers, the oceans and skies the last to be added.

Art aside, the problem with Pola's passion was that Richard was in a relationship with a man. This didn't seem to bother her at all. The family divided up into new configurations and moved away.

Hugo and Hedy

The next house up the driveway looked like a Swiss chalet. In fact, it was. It had been designed by a German Swiss couple named Hugo and Hedy because the view across the valley to the Boney Ridge reminded them of the Alps, without snow. We had pleasant exchanges with both of them as we walked up or down the driveway, but had not shared meals.

One morning when it was barely light, someone was knocking at our front door.

What the heck?

It was a very unusual way to start the day.

It was Hugo. "Have you seen Hedy?"

One of us said, "Well, no, we were sleeping until you knocked. What's going on?"

"She wasn't in her bed when I woke up. I've been walking around the neighborhood calling her name, but I can't find her."

Carl said he would get dressed and help with the search. When he returned after an hour or so, he reported that Hedy had been found by Mike, who lived in the top house on the Knob. She was floating in his swimming pool, dead.

Hugo returned later. "I don't know why she was up there. She didn't know how to swim," he mused, dejectedly.

I asked, "Was she depressed?"

Hugo looked shocked at the thought that she could have committed suicide, but then he offered, "Well, she was very unhappy about how the world was changing around her. And, she hadn't liked seeing Pola sunbathing with no clothes on, right below her garden."

That evening, there was another knock at the front door. Two men in raincoats and hats, *Columbo* look-alikes, asked if they could come in. They were detectives and were investigating the "suspicious death" in the neighborhood.

By now, Erik was almost four. The taller detective asked us if he could speak to Erik first.

"Son, have you noticed anything strange with these neighbors?"

Erik struck a pose, bearing weight on his left leg, with his arms folded across his chest. "Well, I used to see Hedy sweeping the dirt in her front yard with a broom. I thought that was kind of strange."

"Why is that?" the detective asked.

Erik shifted his weight to his right foot and put his hands on his hips.

I could tell he was feeling important being asked these questions.

"Well, there was a cement pathway and stairs to the front door and a bit of grass, which looked very clean. But it was the bare dirt she was sweeping. She said she thought it kept the dust down. I knew because of all the bare dirt around here, she was never gonna get rid of the dust. Maybe that made her sad?"

He must have overheard the earlier conversations, because we had only told him that Hedy had died, not possible causes.

It was never determined what happened to Hedy. Hugo was not held as a suspect for pushing her into the pool. We invited him down for lunch several times. His sister wrote that he could live with her in Switzerland. He put the chalet up for sale. We bought some of his furniture, which was inappropriate for our rugged way of living. Carl later crashed onto the floor when the floral Queen Anne chair gave way. We exchanged Christmas cards for a few years and then didn't hear from him again.

Tom & Tasha

1971 – 1989

"I think John Erik should go to nursery school," Carl said one morning.

"Really? How come?"

"He's here with me while you're at work. He needs kids to play with."

I never went to nursery school, but then I recalled that I grew up in a neighborhood with lots of children. I had planned to stay home with John Erik while Carl worked in his studio, but the nurse Dr. Hodges hired to replace me didn't work out. He called and asked if I could come back. Financially, it was a no-brainer, given the intermittent artist's commissions that found their way to Carl.

My mom drove out to be part of John Erik's initiation of entering the bigger world. We drove to the one-story building just up from Zuma Beach. It looked friendly, with blooming shrubs surrounding it and murals painted on the cement block walls. I held John Erik's right hand, my mom his left and we approached the front door.

A girl with long red hair greeted us.

"Hi! My name is Tasha. I'm four-and-a-half." It appeared she was the official greeter. She was carrying a toy cash register, clutching it to her chest, as if it contained her life's savings. Perhaps it did. She was clearly a nursery school student, but was a head taller than John Erik.

"Follow me," she said officiously. "I'll show ya' around." My mom and I looked at each other, smiled, and followed. John Erik had let go of our hands and we watched him look with wonder at what Tasha pointed to.

"This is where we play with clay and draw. Over here, we have snacks. If we want we can take naps." A nap sounded good to me, but John Erik was darting from place to place.

She motioned for us to follow her behind the school building. "We play ball games here. Sometimes we paint out here so we don't mess up the big room so much."

That seemed reasonable.

We found the head teacher sitting at her desk. She leaned over and kindly asked my son, "What's your name?"

He looked up into her gray eyes and said clearly, "It's John Erik, but I like Erik better."

This was the first time I knew that.

Tasha continued her duties. "Mrs. Johnson, this is Erik's mom and gramma." Tasha turned to us and said, "You can leave now. He'll be fine."

My mom and I looked at each other and at Mrs. Johnson. She smiled. "He will be fine. You can pick him up at 11:45."

My mom and I did what we always did best together. We went to the beach. We didn't have bathing suits with us, but we walked along the water's edge and sat for awhile, looking out at the blue ocean with Catalina in the distance to the south.

It seemed clear we were both aware that this was a new phase for John Erik, because we both had tears in our eyes as we turned and walked to the parking lot. We would lose a bit of him as he made friends and learned skills outside our family.

When we returned at 11:45, Tasha found us right away. "Follow me," she said, swinging her long red tresses to one side and taking ahold of my hand. We walked toward a tall, slender, dark-haired woman.

"This is my mom. Her name is Jennifer." We told her our names while Tasha went to get John Erik.

"Do we have to go home already?" Erik asked. I saw my vision fading that he would stay in our warm home until he went to college.

"We'll come back in two days," I assured him.

"Not tomorrow?" His huge green eyes beseeched me. "But John Erik, don't you think your dad will miss you if you come here every day?"

"Nope. And I want to be called Erik."

It took Carl and me much longer to get used to the idea of Erik being at nursery school, as well as calling him Erik, than it did for him. I think we were supposed to be proud of his easy adaptation. We were…finally.

Jennifer and I sat on the beach a couple of times. She was younger than I was and yet very confident. She explained her ideas of parenting. I felt clueless about how to go about this enormous task of having a child. I was eager to make a new friend.

Some weeks later, Jennifer invited the three of us for dinner. We hadn't met many Malibu folks, so it would be another adventure. Our old friends lived in Venice and Santa Monica. Ruthann and Michael lived in Malibu Canyon, in an area called Monte Nido.

We found Jennifer's house more normal looking than our seven-sided structure with one door, which made me feel anxious.

Tasha opened the front door. "Come on in," she said, as if she were the hostess. The dinner smelled good. The interior of the house did not look as normal as the outside. There was a fair amount of clutter and mismatched furniture, not so different from our house. I felt relieved.

"Go call your dad," Jennifer told Tasha. She did. A very large man entered from a door on the far wall of the living room. I was accustomed to tall people. My dad was six feet, Carl six feet three. But this guy was huge. Maybe six feet eight. He wasn't fat or skinny, just big. He had a ponytail. I watched him approach the table, which was now set with bowls and silverware and a large pot of fragrant chicken and vegetables.

"This is my dad," Tasha said, taking his hand. "His name is Tom." Once again, the familiar first names of her parents instead of just plain dad. He nodded to us and took a seat. His dark eyes twinkled as he made eye contact with Carl and me, but clearly, he was not engaging with Jennifer. He spoke very little. When he finished eating, he nodded to us, and with the faintest smile, disappeared through the far door.

Jennifer noted our discomfort. "Let me explain the situation. Tom and I agreed to raise Tasha until she graduates from high school. But we are separated. We're looking for a place with two buildings so we can be near Tasha, but not each other."

"Oh, my gosh," I blurted, without knowing any of the ramifications that might follow. "I know of just the place...next door to us! The family that had been living there had a similar relationship. The dad lived in the main house with their two sons. The mom lived in a smaller house. They moved out. I think it's available."

"Where is it?" Jennifer asked. I said, "It's where Encinal and Decker Canyons meet. It's called Barney's Knob."

Within a month, Jennifer and Tasha moved into the main house, Tom into the little house. They stayed until Tasha graduated from high school.

Our lives became intertwined for decades, in ways I never anticipated.

Wood

1971

Carl's Easter Island gods and goddesses morphed from wooden chess pieces to salad servers. The first sets of handles resembled the chess pieces, morphed into curvy feminine forms—shoulders, chests, and rumps without arms or legs. They were evocative and Picasso-like and the beginning of grander expressions.

By now, Carl had been laid off from the oil fields in Santa Barbara. He started a boat-bottom cleaning service in order to accumulate tools. He wanted to make art and woodworking was his first medium—or second, if we counted the clay bust of his own head he created several years earlier.

"Tom found wood in San Pedro that he thinks will be good for my sculpting," he told me. "He's gonna take me down there in his truck."

"Okay." I couldn't yet imagine how big the wood would be to require a truck, thinking of chess pieces and salad servers. They turned out to be redwood pilings that were holding up an old bridge in San Pedro which was being dismantled. There were four chunks of redwood, each about twelve feet long and two feet square. Carl had to rent a flatbed trailer to haul them—they were too long for the truck. Somehow, they got the load home and dumped it in the lower lot.

This was looking serious.

In the past, Carl's work and interests were connected to water—as a deckhand, and a sport fishing boat captain, a transporter of workers out to the oil rigs and now the boat-bottom-cleaning business. It appeared that he was moving in a new direction, away from the ocean.

I was always anxious about change and looked at those huge pillars of redwood, wondering what the heck? Totem poles? Tiki gods? We were both generating enough income, so it wasn't the money he spent that concerned me. It was the unknown. We had already deviated from the city-lives of our friends by living in the boondocks, and our lengthy travels to Chile and Denmark—not in each other's company.

What next?

One summer day, I had Erik hoisted on my right hip while we watched wood chips fly out onto the lawn.

"What's it gonna be?" I asked.

"I'm not sure yet."

More chips flew.

I had read somewhere that Michelangelo said the shape he wanted was in the stone. He just had to remove what was superfluous. So, I waited.

The first creature was about eight feet tall, including its pedestal, and was rough-hewn with the chisel marks remaining. It was clearly a female form holding a baby. Something resembling a halo seemed to float above her head.

"So, since you are not exactly churchy or religious, where did the mother/child figure come from?"

"I dunno. That's just how it ended up. Maybe it's you!"

We nicknamed her "The Madonna," and she moved into a corner of the living room, quietly watching over us.

A few months later, the redwood chips were flying again. This one was much more complicated and just as tall. I could see a figure emerging, sitting on its haunches. There were pieces of wood coming out of the top of the head and from under the chin. Delicate arms reached up and below the head with elongated scoops for hands encircling the ends of the rods or sticks.

I knew that patience was part of this artistic adventure, so I quelled my anxiety about the unknown and waited. Now a sanding machine followed the snipping away. And then sandpaper. And then oil. The result was a realistic, yet abstract figure balancing on its toes with slender ankles closely resembling Carl, despite his large torso. The dark redwood was polished until it shone.

"Uh. That's really something," I managed to mutter.

It was beautiful, but it scared me. I could feel the energy coming from the center of the figure. What was trying to pour out of its head.

"I think I'll call it 'Self-Control,'" he said, admiring his creation.

"Of what?" I ventured.

"Oh, maybe fear, or anger, or excitement. Or…I'm not sure. Maybe it's telling me not to be so impulsive," he finished.

That relieved me somewhat, but my own inner energy or demons were so mild I couldn't quite grasp what he might be feeling—despite knowing that he had run away from home when he was fifteen, and later to Chile, after we were married. But then I did know I had not been drawn to my twin, but to my opposite.

For some reason, we called the sculpture "Rolf" instead of "Self-Control." He lived with us for some time until we had to sell him to Carl's father for too low a price when we were short on funds. I missed him. Maybe I figured that as long as those polished wooden hands were holding whatever was bursting to get out, we would be safe.

Two chunks of wood remained in the lower lot. The third one morphed into "Guardian of the Tropopause" some years later. I had to look this up and found it was the boundary in the Earth's atmosphere between the troposphere and the stratosphere. I was glad I learned such a thing existed and was protecting the Earth, and maybe our little house. The sculpture itself was filled with spaces and curves, and no human-type figures emerged from the wood.

I didn't know how Carl had come upon that image either.

A different piece of wood made its way to Barney's Knob from a junkyard in Oxnard. It was about twelve to fifteen feet long and covered with grease. I rued the ten dollar expense and could not imagine what it would become.

The center of our family life is what it became. Once it was sanded, we could see heavy wood, probably oak, laminated together lengthwise. We wondered for years if it had been part of a bowling alley or a pinball machine.

In its first incarnation Carl cut off several feet so it would fit at an angle in our living room/kitchen. He built a sturdy base on which to anchor the now-stunning tabletop. He fashioned stools out of metal tractor seats, which were not comfortable until I covered them with foam and hand-stitched corduroy covers in bright colors. Not furniture for *Architectural Digest*, but still appealing in its own right.

Seven

1972 – 1973

Since Carl had learned to speak Spanish fluently during his sojourn in Chile, he enjoyed being around Spanish-speaking people. He met Francisco at a welding shop in Culver City and asked him if he'd like to come up to our place and work. He agreed.

Over time, Carl helped him get a green card and soon after to make it possible for Francisco's wife, Rosario, to come to the United States from Mexico. We picked her up from the airport. She shyly handed me a package. It was a crocheted shawl—made out of thread, not yarn! The stitches created tiny florets, hundreds of them. Maybe thousands. The shawl was at least six feet long and two feet wide. It was breathtaking. Of course, I cried as I opened it!

Rosario brought their son, Luis, who was about two at the time. Within months, she became pregnant with their second child.

On a Sunday afternoon, we were all gathered around the long, laminated oak table, sipping margaritas. Halfway through the first one, Rosario, who was usually shy and quiet, began waxing poetically about the beauty of having a child.

"*Los niños estan como la spuma de la margarita!*" she said, waving her hands in the air to represent the tiny bubbles coming out of the foam. The children are like the foam of the margarita. "*Ellos traigan la vida, el amor! Necesitas tener mas ninos!*" They bring life and love.

Carl and I looked at each other. Erik was now three and a half. I was approaching thirty and Carl was already there. If we were going to make another baby, it should be sooner than later.

I don't know if it was the *spuma de las margaritas*, or our friends' joy about their own child and pregnancy, but we got up from the table simultaneously and went for my birth-control pills. We took turns punching the little white tablets out of their tinfoil and plastic packaging, and then we flushed them down the toilet with Francisco and Rosario as witnesses.

We did use other methods of birth control for the recommended three months, to allow the birth control hormones to exit my system. Then, on the first try...*bingo*! By this time, Ruthann was pregnant with her first child. The babies' due dates were six weeks apart. This time we attended Lamaze classes.

By now, Carl had been making art out of stained glass, metal, wood and ferrocement on consignment for clients who had found him by word-of-mouth. On a particular request, for a wraparound wine rack with planters, Carl sought out other potters to have the pots made, but none of them were interested in his concept of free-form, non-concentric pots. So, Carl went to the library, got books on making pottery, built a wheel and then a kiln. He fired his first pots the night before the baby's approaching birth. Once again, I worked until the final day of pregnancy, feeling exceptionally good.

My water had broken in the afternoon, two weeks early, but no labor had begun. Ruthann was hosting a baby shower the next day, but our doctor said to come in, because too much time had elapsed since the water had surprised us. Ruthann's baby, David, had also been born two weeks early.

We drove into Santa Monica around midnight. Still no contractions after I was ensconced in my labor bed. The doc arrived and suggested a buccal tablet, Potocin, to get the labor going. The contractions started immediately and violently. I spit the tablet out, because I felt my baby was being pummeled. For my Lamaze focus item, I used a photo of Carl, bandana around his long hair, the impish grin and twinkling eyes, holding his first slumpy pot. The labor continued slowly and gradually increased and Swen was born at 8:44 in the morning. Carl was present for the whole experience and began telling people his baby-birth story to anyone who would listen.

"I tell you, the doctor caught the baby with the grace of a football player!" He was also saddened at what he missed by not being at Erik's birth due to the hospital rules, only four years earlier.

Our helper Barry was living in the studio and stayed with Erik, who began telling callers that he had a new brother named Steve—a name not on my list. We let him keep that for Swen's middle name.

My parents had been traveling in Europe for that year in a camper. My mom had a plane ticket to come home in time for the birth. Barry picked her up at the airport and told her I was busy at work and he would take her home first. When she arrived, Swen was already there…a big surprise. She stayed a few weeks and helped me get through the early, sleep-disturbed nights.

The sleep-disturbed nights did not end for a year.

While Erik followed Dr. Spock's timeline for growth, sleeping and talking to a T, Swen was always off the chart, one way or another. He seemed voraciously hungry and gained pounds each week, instead of ounces.

He wailed when he woke up so that either Carl or Erik would say, "Laura, give him the tit!" The house was small, and it was winter, so there was nowhere to escape during the night.

Time passed. I woke up one morning and saw daylight. I leapt out of bed and picked up Swen and shook him, worried that the reason he hadn't awakened me was that he was dead. He wasn't. His big blue eyes looked at me as if to say, "Why the heck are you shaking me?"

Swen's talking came late. My mom said it was because Erik took care of him and could intuit his needs, so he didn't need to say much! His contagious, wide smile made up for the sleepless nights and my wondering what he was thinking or feeling.

Ruthann and I traded our babies for a free day each week. We met at the Old Place on Mulholland, halfway between our homes. She would take Swen for a full day, and on another day I would bring David home with me. These days were lifesaving for both of us, maybe all four of us. I used most of my free days to sleep, but as time went on, I became fully human again. I only worked for Dr. Hodges on occasional days when Smokey or Margaret needed time off.

Except for not sleeping through the night for a year, I loved being at home with Swen and getting Erik ready for school. He merely had to hike across the vacant lot next door, to Decker Road where he got on and off the school bus. Once Swen was walking, he loved to stand at the edge of the driveway when the bus pulled up, wave his arms and call out, "Eyah! Eyah!" as soon as he saw his big brother.

Yoga & Toni
1973

In 1973, once I had recovered from Swen's birth and that first year of non-sleep, I was ready to return to belly dance classes. Without my giant belly, I could start making my hip girdle and add even more sparkling sequins and clanking coins.

But the gas crisis had begun. One had to purchase gas on odd or even days, depending on the last number of your license plate, and the lines of waiting went around the block or up the street. Van Nuys was over thirty miles for me and over twenty for Patsy—one way. The math seemed to indicate an increase in long lines, and we decided to wait and see when it would stop.

At the same time, Ruthann told me she had been reading about yoga and wanted to start going to a class. Did I know of one? My new friend Gale did. It met on Tuesday mornings at the Malibu West Swim Club, less than ten miles from home. I decided to join them, even though my picture of yoga was slow, foreign and didn't have peppy music and moves. But there were those gas lines….

The first few weeks were uneventful, just getting used to the postures I had never done— some easier, some more difficult, especially the headstand. The teacher's name was Toni. She had a slender, wiry frame and could do everything without effort. I think she was in her fifties, which seemed quite old to be doing such intense movements. I was intrigued when she mentioned which internal organs were stimulated by specific postures—the Shoulder Stand caused the neck to fold forward, stimulating the thyroid, and the Fish moved the neck backward, stimulating the parathyroid glands. My Western medical training had not provided any prophylactic guidance aiming toward better health. At UCLA, a big teaching hospital, most of the patients I cared for had been sick with complicated diseases, many of them remaining there for months and even years. At times, I imagined I would be dead by thirty, like a number of patients I had cared for. Yoga—helping one remain healthy—this was a new concept for me. And I liked it.

Due to requests from her students, Toni had added a twenty minute meditation time at the end of the class. Before we became quiet and focused on our breaths—another new concept for me—she usually offered a brief pearl of wisdom. Sometimes it would be about meditation.

"Just feel how cool the breath is as it goes up your right nostril and comes out your left," she might say.

Could my two nostrils behave separately from one another?

Other times it was more, well, maybe metaphysical. Or out to lunch, like: "After death, the souls circle the earth until it is time for them to reincarnate. Then they select their parents for their next life."

Hmmm, there was that reincarnation word again.

I hadn't read any of the books Pola suggested.

Ruthann and I would look at each other and roll our eyes. (Toni's eyes were closed so she couldn't see us.) But in about six months, when I could stand on my head without the wall as support, and I could feel a cool sensation in my nose, even if it was in both nostrils, Toni's ideas didn't seem so crazy.

Ruthann and I might say, "So that doesn't sound so weird, but let's not discuss it with Michael and Carl." We were happy to be learning new concepts, and we were definitely feeling healthier and more limber, even though the class only met one hour each week. Despite the brief exposure to Toni, her influence was lifelong. The combination of the yoga postures, meditation and Eastern points of view provided a platform for growth throughout the rest of my life.

About a year and a half into this new experience, Toni announced that she was leaving Malibu to follow her guru. We found out that this included leaving her husband and teenage children, which was a bit shocking to me. The whole guru concept was foreign. I had read *The Autobiography of a Yogi* by this time, but I didn't get from it that one should drop everything. Yogananda had a spiritual teacher who he followed, but he didn't have a family to leave behind, nor a yoga class upon which we had all become rather dependent.

A woman named Suzanne and I took over the class, alternating weeks. We did the same routine we had learned from Toni, even though neither of us had formal training. It didn't seem to bother anyone. Yoga had become indispensable to both Ruthann and me, as well as the others who continued coming to the class for over five years.

I never did make it back to Everywoman's Village.

Moving Next Door
1974

Shortly after Swen turned one, Patsy's mom visited. She looked at our little house, which I thought of as cozy, and asked, "Why don't you live over there where there is much more room?"

After Phine moved out, Carl started using the room on the west as his pottery studio. In the cold weather, it also served as a chicken coop. With their cages hoisted up to the ceiling near the fluorescent lights, they laid eggs all winter.

I had taken over the north room for sewing, plus we found a claw-footed bathtub that sat in that space for family use. But we continued living in the little house. It had not occurred to me to move to the collection of modules because they still seemed so ugly. But the thought had life, and we began planning the move.

During the night, to avoid any California Coastal Commission helicopters from spotting building-without-permit projects, Carl built a roof on the open deck that connected the three modules. At a recycling outlet he found antique windows with wavy glass and diamond-shaped panes across the top. They enclosed the far end of what now looked like a room. One of his artistically designed metal fireplaces sat in front of the row of windows. He also found two sturdy doors with opaque glass windows, which resembled dental or medical office doors from the fifties. They became the front door, and the back door, with panes of glass enclosing the space on either side of the doors. It was beginning to feel like a real house.

January rolled around again, when we always seemed to move, my least favorite thing ever. We had lived in the little house for five years, and despite the cramped space in the winter when we couldn't use the screen porch, I was happy with my "cottage." My mother called it a shack.

Even though we only had to move across the lawn, I was anxious and exhausted. We had to figure out how to switch the pottery materials to the little house, our bed to the pottery room, the bunk beds to the north room and where to put the long laminated oak table that we had been gathering around for several years. Carl solved that problem by knocking down the kitchen cabinets and the Formica kitchen counter and placing the oak plank on it.

It was perfect.

It was especially perfect when Carl called me into the new kitchen after I was whining about the move and the stuff and that I was tired and….

"Here. Climb up on the counter." He had towels laid out and a chair placed at the end holding a big pot of water, with steam wafting upward.

"What's this?" I asked.

"Number one, I'm going to calm you down and spruce you up. I can see how wiped out you are from the move. Number two, I'm going to fulfill your hair-washing scene from "Out of Africa."

I managed to hoist myself up on the counter and onto my back. Carl wrapped the towel around my neck and shoulders and scooted me up to the edge. I had so loved the scene where Robert Redford washed Meryl Streep's hair that I thought it took up most of the film. In later re-watches, it lasted less than two minutes.

Carl slowly poured the warm water over my head, a cup at a time,, followed by the shampoo and gentle massaging of my head and hair. I kept my eyes closed, both to keep out the shampoo, but also to imagine that it was Robert Redford washing my hair. Actually, Carl was more handsome than Robert, but still. Then, more rinsing with more warm water and the towel wrapped around my head. There was a twin bed in the kitchen we had found for my mom to sleep on when she came for Swen's birth, since there was no room for her to sleep in the little house. Carl led me to the bed, and wrapped my head again in dry towels. I was in heaven. I figured I could continue living and manage to put our belongings into their new shelves and closets. I slept for a while.

Swen toddled over and nuzzled me. "Hi Momma," he said. We were both turning into sweet souls, now that we were getting a full night's sleep.

Despite not sleeping through the night and not talking in full sentences, he was ahead of his milestones physically. He walked before one and could climb…onto everything: the counter, once we attached stools to the floor, the fridge, the top bunk bed and later, our van. This also meant he fell often because his judgment was not as developed as his strength. The three of us rescued him frequently when he hollered for help.

Charmlee, the "Flateau," and The Cave

Now that we were living on the edge of the cliff, we looked across the canyon to a long, knoll that stretched almost to the ocean. In those years, we took the old Land Rover to a dirt road Carl found and drove to the end of it. We could walk and walk and see different views in various directions. Swen could still ride in a pack on Carl's back. Erik ran around everywhere with great energy. We found the footprint of a house—only the front steps and the chimney remained. The couple's names were scratched into the cement step: Charmian and Lee. There was a large, empty reservoir. We were told they ran cattle at one time. This ridge was later donated to the county and became Charmlee Park, with a proper entrance and parking lot one mile down Encinal Canyon from our driveway.

Once people found out about it, there was talk of baseball diamonds and playgrounds. But the majority of the community ruled against it. And the park stayed natural with only walking trails. On the eastern border were enormous boulders—it felt like being in Utah or Arizona. Out at the end and to the northwest we could see the Channel Islands, Anacapa, Santa Cruz and on clear days, Santa Rosa and San Miguel. Straight ahead loomed whale-shaped Santa Barbara Island, and to the south, Catalina.

In the middle of the park stretched a vast meadow filled with wildflowers in the spring. Before county ownership, there was a herd of wild horses that roamed the meadow which we enjoyed watching, and we were sad to see them go once the land became public. The south border was filled with oak groves. I found a place I liked to sit where I could look past the meadow, all the way to the Boney Ridge. The vistas were spectacular and endless.

We also had more time to hike out from our house. The land next to us had been flattened to accommodate helicopters during wildfires. Erik and Swen referred to it as "The Flateau." It was owned by one of the retired firemen, and he didn't mind the kids playing there or us walking across it to the cave.

Our landlord's children had created a trail that went from the flateau, across the ridge, down into a gulley, and up to the rocky peak we could see from our home. Once on top of the peak, it was a steep and rocky climb, first down, and then up to a small cave. It was possible to fit three to four people in the cave, sitting cross-legged and upright. The opening perfectly framed Catalina, stretching from the west end, to the isthmus and to Avalon. It was a place to come alone for solace, or to hike to with friends. We considered it our own.

Blue Sky
1974 – 1979

THE BLUE SKY POTTERY SALES AND CAFE

As Carl's pottery developed in style and quality, we decided to have pottery sales at home. I made flyers and mailed them to everyone we knew and placed them around town in shops and on bulletin boards. RSVPs started coming in. At the first couple of gatherings, we served popcorn and apple cider. The response increased, and it seemed to be turning into a social event. People began to ask us when the next one would take place. I decided to up the ante and provide some real food. Ever since reading *The Bobbsey Twins at the Ice Palace,* I had envisioned running a hotel and restaurant. Now was a chance to practice.

I wrote up a list of objects for Carl to make: wine goblets, carafes and bowls for fruit, which he was already making, crocklets for butter and wooden breadboards. I added crude drawings of my lunch vision on the next sale flyer. It advertised a carafe of wine, homemade multigrain bread, cheese and butter and a bowl of fruit for a whopping $2.50 per person—reservations seriously required.

The patio with the spectacular view still had a dirt floor. We gathered together card tables, boards and sawhorses, and as many funky chairs as we could rustle up. My mom made blue and white checkered tablecloths, which helped a great deal to unite the conglomeration of furniture. We had a couple of garden umbrellas, which also helped with the ambiance. I baked a dozen loaflets of wholegrain, wheat berry bread the previous day.

Patsy and Frank came up the day before the event to help us get ready for the great experiment. We woke up in the morning and found fog completely enveloping our house, the patio and the view. It was disappointing to say the least. Patsy and I forged ahead anyway, setting the tables and hanging Carl's pottery from the pine tree branches.

About two hours later, the fog changed its mind and started rolling down the canyon. Patsy hollered to all of us, "Look! It's the Blue Sky Cafe!" It was indeed, and the name Blue Sky stuck to all our activities for decades.

The guests arrived and chose their tables. Once a few sips of wine were imbibed, I don't think anyone noticed the dirt floor or the rickety tables and chairs.

It was a success.

Word spread. Ruthann joined Patsy and me as waitresses. My mom made cool, long aprons for each of us. Carl cemented the patio floor and we gathered or made better tables and chairs. At its height, the cafe ladled out seventy-five lunches on one day, served in shifts. Some people even requested specific tables and asked for Reserved signs to be posted!

The Blue Sky Boutique

Carl had clearly become a potter now, leaving behind the stained glass and steel. The home sales were good, but a lot of work, and the income was sporadic. What if we had a permanent shop? I was also getting antsy staying on the mountain all the time. Carl said, "If it makes you happy to be out and about, it will be worth it, whether it is profitable or not."

Perhaps I had become a bit grumpy and lonely.

A new shopping center had been built on Point Dume. It provided a market, bank, restaurant, bakery, hair salon and hardware store. Beneath an already large Chinese elm tree stood a wooden structure, not quite a gazebo… it was a rectangle…and not exactly a trellis. I guess it was placed there for architectural accent, and it had possibilities.

Our contractor friend Bill had become an avid fan of Carl's work, buying a dozen or so freestanding fireplaces for his newly built homes. He also bought The Madonna sculpture. Bill took a look at the structure and said he could glass it in and put a roof on it with no problem. We contacted the manager of the center who thought it was a good idea, another place for her to garner income.

Bill got to work, and Carl and his helper Gabriel welded hanging racks with wooden shelves and stoneware corners framing each opening. Beneath the shelves were low cupboards for storage. Carl fashioned a long, dark, wood table with metal bands holding the planks together.

Sitting behind this table is where I would hold court for the next five years.

We enrolled Swen in the nursery school across the street, along with his best friend Amber, who lived down the canyon a bit. I made arrangements with a local greenhouse owner to buy plants at wholesale to enhance the stoneware pots. Our friend, Ronnie, made a sign on a large wooden plank shaped like a cloud. The letters were slightly misaligned, so some people asked if it was called Blue The Sky Boutique, but most people understood what the name was. Gale's husband, Don, created a logo and made postcard-size business cards that I could mail to customers when their orders were ready.

We began moving the pottery and plants into the framed spaces, and in February of 1975 had a grand opening. A newspaper photographer was there taking pictures. Our friends came. New customers showed up and started buying right away. In addition to pots, there were plates, goblets, bowls and coffee mugs.

It turned out there was a local guru whose followers lived close by and wanted to honor him with gifts. So I added crystals, rainbow-y cards and heart-shaped items. I had a thriving business with them alone! The ten-by-fifteen foot space sparkled with the lush green Chinese elm graciously spreading its leaves overhead to provide shade and coolness.

The art, plants and twinkling crystals must have provided a magical aura because almost daily someone occupied the chair across from me and told me their stories. Friends who were happily married—I thought—told me about affairs and yearnings for travel and change, which they never mentioned in other settings. Total strangers asked if they could just sit awhile. Some said they were on their way to Zuma Beach and stopped at the center to buy food when they were drawn to my little shop. I was in heaven. It had been well over two years since I left Dr. Hodges' office, and I had begun to miss the patients and my co-workers. I was a social being and loved the company and the atmosphere.

I wish I had thought about being a writer back then. I would have taken notes about the stories that were so generously shared.

The Big Actor, or A Black Cloud over the Blue Sky

Not all days were peace and bliss. We had made friends with an actor after Carl built some bookcases and light fixtures for him. We attended his wedding. He joined us at one of our lamb roasts, plus we shared dinners and brunches. He had a reputation for having a temper, but our interactions with him had been fun and he was very kind to us, maybe because he was pleased to have friends who were not in the film world, and he had no reason to strut. When he had asked at a recent dinner party about haircutters in town, I had told him about the one across from the boutique.

One day, he filled the frame of the sliding glass door of the boutique. I looked up and could see he was angry. Seething, in fact.

"I just had my hair cut at that salon and the 'screaming queen' charged me twenty bucks! I only have four strands of hair left and told him it wasn't worth twenty dollars, and gave him ten and left." His face was red; his huge shoulders were clenched. I sat quietly and surreptitiously glanced at the woman in the chair opposite who happened to be an actress and knew him.

Then I heard the voice of the hairdresser, although I couldn't see him behind the actor's bulk. "Laura, this guy won't pay for his haircut and wouldn't give me his phone number so I could tell my boss."

Suddenly the actor turned and grabbed the hairdresser by the back of the neck and tossed him across the patio. The hairdresser scrambled as fast as he could to keep from doing a face-plant on the cement. I started crying. The actor came in and tried to hug me. The actress sat still and quiet.

The actor left, apologizing for upsetting me but not for what he did.

Within hours two policemen arrived and asked me for the actor's name and phone number. I told them I couldn't do that because he was a family friend and I felt I would be betraying him. They convinced me that if I didn't give the information, they would spot him on the highway and pull him over and handcuff him and it would be worse than if they peacefully knocked on his door.

I succumbed and cried more.

Two days later the phone rang. It was the actor. He yelled about our friendship and how I betrayed him after he had been so kind to us. I tried to explain what the cops said, but he had no room for that. I also pointed out there was a witness in the boutique who knew him and she would have given out his information, too. I was devastated and finally hung up.

That wasn't the end of it. The hairdresser hired an attorney and sued for physical damages. I was summoned to a deposition in Beverly Hills. The actor sat across from me and glared. I never did hear how the lawsuit was settled.

Entertainment

Fortunately, there was way more fun than trauma at the boutique. Gale and I rustled up a festive book-signing party there for our friend Bob Specht's book, *Tisha*. The story took place in Alaska, so we found a couple who played banjos and sang. There was food, wine, laughter, music and lots of guests strolling, eating and buying his books.

On regular occasions, Jonathan Winters would appear and do a regular TV monologue right in the midst of the tiny shop. It was a bit overwhelming—his voice was loud, his expression intense—but he always made us laugh.

My most enjoyable experiences in the Blue Sky Boutique were the stories told, the people I met, the opportunity to hang out in an artful setting and friends I made—many of whom have stayed with me the rest of my life.

Who'd-a-thought so much could happen in a one hundred and fifty square-foot glass house?

Cultural Adventures

1975 - 1985

Juanita

Francisco and Rosario didn't come out so often anymore. Having two children to look after and Francisco's full-time job limited their weekend excursions. But, they did introduce us to Juanita. We saw that with my working at the boutique, nursery school was helpful, but we needed more care for Swen, and Mexican meals sounded good.

We created a sleeping space for her in my office. She was very gracious and appreciative for small things. She loved that we included her when we sat down to eat because other households had not done that. She loved telling us stories while we ate, and often used her napkin as a prop, rolling it into a tube, flattening it or folding it. Our days went along smoothly. She lived with us for almost two years, until Ruthann and Michael's second child, Adam, was born. Then Juanita moved to their house.

Coyote

Gabriel was a tall, slender Zapotecan who came to work for Carl. He moved into the old screen porch. He told us he was married…no children, yet… and would like to find a way for his wife to join him. Since he didn't have a green card, she couldn't simply get on a plane and fly here.

One night, my friend Eileen was having dinner with me. Juanita was cooking her special chile rellenos for us when someone knocked at the front door. It was a Mexican man who spoke fairly clear English. He pointed to his truck and said he had a woman in the back. Eileen and I looked at each other with raised eyebrows and followed him down the front steps.

He opened the rear door of the truck and pulled the tailgate down. After moving some boxes out into the yard, he lifted a sheet of plywood. There, curled up in a ball was indeed a woman. She looked up at us, her dark eyes either in shock or fear. By this time, Eileen and I were gaping. It took the woman some time to straighten her legs. We could see she had naturally curly hair, which was fluffed way out like a lion with a dye job, and was peppered with what looked like sawdust.

Finally, she was able to ease her way out onto the tailgate, and then gingerly, onto the ground, where she stood as she tried to get her bearings.

I welcomed her—I knew it had to be Gabriel's wife, Enedina—though we weren't expecting her.

"Vamos," I said. *"Necesitamos andar poquito por circulación."* We need to walk a bit to improve your circulation. My Spanish was useful but not grammatically correct. I held onto her arm as we walked around the yard while the man—clearly a coyote—used the bathroom and got some water. Neither Carl nor Gabriel were on the Knob. I didn't know what would happen when the moment for payment came up.

"So, did you drive all the way across the border with her in the back?" I asked. It was at least a three, if not four-hour drive, depending on where they started in Mexico.

"Si, como no?" Like, how else would I get her here? he said.

Just then, Gabriel drove in. We watched him embrace his wife and introduce her to us. Then he settled up with the coyote, who reloaded the boxes, closed the truck and drove away.

I knew this kind of transport was going on all the time, but I had never seen up-close-and-personal what it takes to get to the United States if you did not have documentation.

Eileen and I returned to the kitchen and sat down to eat the rellenos.

Juanita asked, *"Que pasó?"* I knew she had been standing behind the screen door watching the activities, but didn't want me to have noticed that. I described the situation the best I could, and then to Carl, who arrived soon after.

CHICHARRONES

Gabriel and Enedina settled in to the screen porch. When winter came, we stapled clear plastic sheets onto the screen panels to keep the rain out. One day, he asked if he could have a birthday party here. Of course. We liked birthdays and we liked parties.

Several men arrived in the afternoon and placed a copper pot onto the patio. It must have been four feet in diameter and at least that tall. Other men arrived with a pig carcass, which they began cutting into small pieces of meat. The fat was put into the pot first. As the sun went down, the meat was tossed into the pot and they took turns stirring it with what we later called the chicharron paddle. And then the rain started.

By now, there were many women in the kitchen, gathered around the oak countertop. They were chopping tomatoes, onions and cilantro on one end of the counter. At the other end, women were stirring masa into dough, while another group stood at the stove making tortillas. Lots of tortillas. They were kept warm in the oven.

Rain started dripping onto the counter, which had never happened before. I saw a quick fix and climbed onto the counter with some paper plates that I taped over the leak. Duct tape might have solved the problem, but it was likely I used Scotch tape. In about thirty minutes dripping water landed on the counter and the food, but not enough water to drench everyone around the counter.

This did not daunt the ladies. They laughed heartily, and we moved the cutting and chopping operation to the dining room table, where there were no leaks…yet.

Soon, the men came into the house, wet but in good humor. Likely tequila had been passed around outside, as it was inside. They carried platters of crispy chicharrones and carnitas. We created a buffet of the meat, salsa, and freshly-made tortillas. It was the best possible food.

By now the living room was filled with children running around, a granny snuggled on the couch, and many people holding paper plates filled with carnitas tacos. Mexican music had been playing throughout the evening.

Suddenly, a very large woman stood up and the room quieted. Her black hair was almost down to her waist. Her eyes were twinkling, and it seemed everyone but me knew what would happen next.

She started singing. Really singing. With an operatic quality voice, tender love songs, folk ballads. It was so beautiful and so unexpected that of course, Patsy and I started crying.

Then Gabriel stood up. He clasped his hands behind his back and began shuffle steps to the corrida music. Other men and women joined him, including me. It was easy to follow.

Babies and toddlers were starting to fall asleep, along with the granny, despite the singing and shuffling. Bit by bit, the people packed up and went home.

It was possibly the best birthday party I ever attended.

It also may have started what my family called Mexican Night—standing around the oak counter cutting up veggies and meat, playing Jorge Negrete and Miguel Acevejas.

We never did figure out how to make fresh tortillas.

SERBIA

Patsy's parents were both from Serbia. We often went out to their home in Pomona, which had a larger than normal yard, filled with chickens, goats, vegetables and fruit trees. We gathered there for Serbian Christmases and Easters, always a week later than those holidays we were accustomed to, so we got to enjoy both.

Nada, Patsy's mom, was famous for many things, but especially for making strudel, which was called pita. It was more like filo dough. I watched her make it one time. She started with a large ball of dough in the center of the dining room table, which was covered with a floured sheet used for that purpose only. She then slid her hands under the dough, tucked her fingers toward the ceiling, and started circling the table, again and again, each time the dough becoming thinner and reaching toward the edge of the table. Finally, the paper-thin dough almost reached the floor. It was mesmerizing to watch. Then she spread long rows of walnuts, cinnamon and raisins and started rolling them, cutting when there were enough layers and the roll could fit into the oven. She also made long rows of cheese or ground meat—some for appetizers, some for dessert.

We attended three Serbian weddings, one Baptism and one funeral. These were festive occasions with the above-mentioned pita, lamb dishes, salads and slivovitz, a Serbian brandy. "Nostrovya!" Live musicians played at the weddings, and we danced the *kolo* and sang, "Miserlu."

The Egg Wars also started from a Serbian tradition. Its original version was for two people, each holding a boiled Easter egg, and then smacking the tip of the egg against their opponent's egg to see which egg cracked first.

This morphed into an annual extravagant creation, mainly between Carl and Frank. Over the years, there was the ICBEgg, Egg of Nazareth, Muamar Egg, The Roman Pit-fighting Egg, The Motating Jungle War Egg, Herbie the Killer Egg, Egg-o-Rama and Egg of Troy.

The grand finale took place in 1984. Carl and the boys stayed up late creating the Chinese Chicken War Egg. It was a wooden construction covered with plastic wrap, fierce eyes and giant red lips. The egg was at least five feet in diameter. They carried it up to Tom's and hid it behind trees, then strung a rope from Tom's yard to the far end of our lawn. At the moment of the contest, Frank did his display, the Ass-Kicking Eggolator, which in all previous years would have won. And then music started playing and the giant egg was set loose, floating and swaying over the canyon until it landed on the lawn. The crowd cheered, laughed and hollered.

My mother later said, "It's no wonder Carl left home—he knew he could never top the Chinese Chicken War Egg."

Chile/North Africa

Carl and I listened to KPFK radio when working in the shop. A weekly program was created by Carlos Hagen, a Chilean, who discussed various topics, interspersed with music. Because of Carl's sojourn to Chile in 1967, he was especially interested in Carlos's comments on the political upheaval in Chile in the seventies.

One day, I was sitting in the boutique when a dark-complexioned man strolled in and looked with interest at every piece of pottery. When I asked if I could help him and he responded, I knew immediately who it was, owing to his accent and way of speaking.

"Are you Carlos Hagen?" I ventured.

"Why, yes, I am," he said with a slight stutter.

"We listen to your program every week. My husband Carl went to Chile in 1967 and would be thrilled to meet you. Can you come up for dinner?"

"Wouldn't that be an imposition?" he inquired.

"Not at all. I'll call Carl and ask him to cook a dinner for a surprise guest."

He followed me home and this began a decade of ethnic gatherings. He invited interesting friends from KPFK and from UCLA, where he ran the map library. We invited our friends. The oak counter was surrounded by people, cutting and chopping vegetables or making and rolling out dough. Sometimes we made empanadas, a Chilean version of tacos with a cinnamon flavor. On other Sunday afternoons, we made couscous. Carlos had gifted us with a couscoussier, a large pot in which a vegetable and lamb stew was cooked in the bottom. A second layer of the pot had holes, small enough to contain the couscous grain, but large enough to allow the steam from the stew to waft up and cook the couscous, infusing its flavors.

Carlos brought ethnic music from his vast collection of thousands of LP albums. He had so many that he built a two-story cement bunker in his yard to house them. I made curtains for the bunker windows in exchange for some of the records.

Denmark

My mother was not Danish, but she learned to cook *frikedeller,* Danish meatballs, red cabbage and parsley new potatoes. But it wasn't until I visited Denmark in 1967 that I learned the art of the *frokost*. This meal consisted of open-faced sandwiches in courses, accompanied by acquavit, a potato-based liqueur and beer. The meal started with herring and onion on pumpernickel—after smearing the bread with butter—or white bread with a butter lettuce leaf filled with tiny shrimp, a dollop of mayonnaise, paprika and a lemon slice. Every few bites were followed by a shooter of acquavit, during which the guests were required to make eye contact with everyone else, and then chase it with beer.

The next course included various meats such as sausage—*mediste pølse*—thinly sliced pork or headcheese. These were served on pumpernickel with garnishes of mustard and Tilsit, Havarti or Danablu—on white bread decorated with radish florets. Coffee and cakes followed.

The remarkable thing is that with so much alcohol, I never saw anyone appear to be drunk. There might be laughter and sometimes singing, but no sloppiness or anger. Except for one time when a guest brought marijuana cookies. That didn't end well. But, that is another story.

Ideas Brewing

1975 and on...

Often, Carl picked me up at the boutique after I had pedaled my bike down the mountain in the morning. One evening we sat there longer, maybe enjoying an extra glass of wine. We got to chatting about our kitchen.

I opined, "How could they have placed the kitchen facing the spectacular view, with two small windows up high? You have to stand up to look out."

Carl responded, "Well that's how it is," not chiming in with his usual creative ideas.

I continued some more, maybe whining by now. "Couldn't we find some bigger windows?" He looked pensive.

I could see his wheels turning.

"Let's go," he said. I drove home, too fast, the wine guiding us.

Carl entered the kitchen with some hefty crowbars. My heart leapt into my throat. This was looking different than installing some larger windows. The buildings had been assembled with four-by-eight plywood sheets on the outside. The kitchen was the only room that had internal paneling, more of the ugly brown stuff, which I had already painted yellow.

He stuck a crowbar in between two panels. "Here. Help me pull it!"

I did.

A deafening crack sounded as the panel ripped halfway off the wall. After the two inner panels were removed, we turned to the west-facing plywood sheets. More ripping sounds. It was already transforming!

We moved to the south-facing wall—two more panels and two more sheets of plywood. The influence of the wine must have worn off, because if we had stepped over the threshold in either direction we would have fallen five feet to the west, and eight feet to the south.

We both grabbed hold of the corner post and hung on and leaned out. We were giggling by now at the spaciousness that had developed.

"Oh my God!" I shrieked. We could look straight ahead and see stars and the outline of the cascading mountains. If we looked up, we could see a quarter moon and the plane of the ecliptic, planets wending their way from east to west. It was spectacular.

We turned the kitchen chairs onto their sides to block the openings in case the boys got up before we did. Then we went to bed.

In the morning, after looking out while we sipped our coffees and munched our toast, Carl left for the hardware store to buy screen. I filled the staple-gun, my most treasured tool. By noon the area was screened in. It was summer, and we figured we could leave it like that until the rains came.

Within a year, a screen porch was added to the southern open space, and stairs were built down into the patio. Then, I requested French doors. Carl had Gabriel weld two sets of doors with glass panels out of steel. I called them Polish doors, instead of French…not quite as graceful as I had pictured, but they worked. I painted them royal blue.

When friends walked in the front door of the house, they were suddenly transported out into the canyon. It was gasp-able.

Brunch with Staff

The December following the opening of the Blue Sky Boutique, I invited my "staff" to have brunch at The Wine Cellar. By staff I meant the pals who sat in the boutique for a day each week to give me a day off, in addition to Sunday. This gathering included Eileen, Judy, Dona, Sandra and Ruthann. I wanted to thank them for helping me, which they did for free.

We were seated in the patio beneath the feathery pepper tree, clinking our wine glasses around the table. Stories were shared about the remarkable collection of customers who wandered into the little glassed-in building and who sat in the second oak chair. It was almost as if the chair elicited truth serum. It happened with everyone.

My left elbow was being nudged. It was my friend Gale, with her husband Don. They were seated next to our slightly rowdy group. We did reach-across hugs, and everyone greeted them, and we continued with our stories.

Gale nudged me again. I turned toward her and saw she was slightly teary. I took hold of her hand.

"I just wanted to tell you how ashamed I am about my behavior at the party the other night."

Several of our married circle had recently separated and were in a divorce group together. Gale had approached another friend of ours and said, "Harriet, you really need to get yourself in that group. It's really helping those ladies." Harriet said, "But I don't like groups, and I don't want to go." Gale followed up with something like, "Well, you're cooking your own goose," and stomped away from Harriet. I stood there with my jaw hanging open, not knowing what to say to Harriet or Gale. So I said nothing and drank some more wine.

By now Gale was weeping. "It is like some spirit enters me and I blurt things out without thinking about the effect of my words. I have been working on this my whole adult life, so it shocks me when I hear myself do it again. I hope you will forgive me."

I had continued holding her hand and took hold of her other hand. By now I was weeping too, because I knew this was a very difficult thing for her to realize and then to share. I knew at that moment we would be friends forever because of her honesty and desire to become a better person.

"Gale, this doesn't even need forgiving by me. You are forgiving yourself by telling me what you are realizing and feeling."

"Thank you," she said.

I said, "Thank you!" I knew it was a rare moment.

She turned toward Don and I returned to my staff, ready to eat a delicious brunch, knowing I had a new true friend.

We are still friends, forty-plus years later.

The Wedge

We were at The Wine Cellar with our husbands on Ruthann's first night out after giving birth to Adam, her second son. She had recovered from the birth and caught up on the missed sleep. And, she had gotten a new haircut.

It was 1976, the year Dorothy Hamill won everything on ice at the

Olympics. She also got a haircut. It was called The Wedge and everyone was getting one. Except me. My hair didn't have that kind of body. But Ruthann's did. She had the best hair ever: thick and stiff, but curvy and an ashy blond color that remained into almost old age.

Of course, we were having some wine with our dinner and chatting about our families.

I suddenly noticed Carl and Michael were just gazing at Ruthann. She was glowing. Her always-beautiful clear skin was plumped up by motherhood. And that hair, the best Wedge in the country. I doubt that our husbands even knew what it was called, but I did. I felt jealous, sad, ignored and not very pretty. My higher mind was telling me my feelings were ridiculous, but there they were. I was having a hard time eating. But why would I feel this way? Now we both had two sons and would continue our co-parenting. I got quiet and tried to be gracious when one of the guys, or maybe both, said, "Look at Ruthann! Doesn't she look great?" I wanted to say she always looks great, snappishly, but fortunately didn't. I smiled the best I could, but remained quiet all the way home.

"What's up?" Carl asked on the drive home. I was rarely at a loss for words.

"Oh, nothing. I'm fine." I was too embarrassed to say what I had been feeling.

Recently, I had begun noticing how critical I was of myself, likely inherited from my mom who was critical of *herself*. As much as she loved me, she said and did things that implied I needed to change something about myself, like what I chose to wear, or how to cut my hair. Or more likely not cutting my hair—she did not like long hair on anyone.

I made a silent pledge to be more aware of my internal attitude, which was sometimes self-supportive, yet often self-destructive.

Bob & Carol & Ted & Alice

1975

Things were going well. The boutique was bringing in more regular income than ever before. I loved my days there, listening to varied stories from whomever stopped by. Swen had adjusted to the nursery school across the street from the boutique. Erik was in the second grade and had a teacher he liked. We were making new friends, keeping the old and having fun-filled gatherings.

The calm before the storm? The deep breath before the plunge?

On a summer morning, we wandered outside with our coffee cups to find two seeming-to-be strangers camped on the lawn. They wiggled out of their sleeping bags and greeted us.

"I am John, your cousin," the fellow informed Carl, "and this is my wife, Debbie." She offered a grin that was toothier than my own.

The light bulb finally went on in Carl's gaze.

"Wow! We haven't seen each other since we were all children. How did you find us here?"

"My dad knew where your mom was. We planned this road trip through California and thought it would be cool to meet you again."

"Well, welcome! Do you want some coffee? Or to use the bathroom?"

"Sure." They followed us into the house.

Carl's mom, Virginia, happened to be staying with us as well, not a frequent happening. She was intrigued to meet her long-lost nephew, too. For awhile, anyway.

I never did understand why the family was so out of touch with each other. While I didn't see my cousins much, other than at Christmas since we had started creating our own families, I always knew where they were and how they were.

We fixed breakfast for everyone and shared bits of our lives. They didn't have children. They were in touch with his sisters but didn't see them much. I learned nothing about the wife's family. Maybe I sensed something discomforting and didn't ask. She didn't ask me about mine, either. She was a very skilled artist, and she spent time that afternoon with Carl in his studio carving hands and fish on some of his large platters. It was impressive work.

It was a Sunday, and Patsy and Frank were coming up to say hi to Carl's mom, share a BBQ dinner with us and spend the night. Frank remembered Carl's cousin from his childhood years, growing up in Carl's hometown. The dinner went well.

As usual, Patsy and I conked out earlier than the guys. I went to bed. Patsy curled up somewhere, and Virginia made it to the sleeping quarters we had rigged up for her.

Sometime during the night, I woke up and both Frank and Carl were in our big bed, one on either side of me, snoring like crazy. This had never happened before, but they were too far drunk to ask them "what the heck?" In addition to smelling like booze, there was a strong fragrance of dried grass wafting about this very odd arrangement.

In the morning, the atmosphere was strained and just plain weird. Virginia was not her smiley/giggly self, a relief in some ways, but clearly a signal something was off. Patsy was outside with a cup of coffee. Carl and Frank looked hungover and were not very chatty. We made breakfast and the newfound cousins bid us adieu. I wasn't clear what was going on, but it was creepy.

Patsy and Frank left after awhile, and Carl and I took naps and hung out with Erik and Swen. No conversation took place.

The next day I came home from the boutique. Carl greeted me with "We need to talk."

He brought two short glasses of something with ice cubes and we sat on the couch.

"So?" I queried.

Carl started talking with a shaky voice, not his usual he-man timbre. "Debbie and John have an open marriage, and they say it is working very well for them. I am just not made to be a one-woman man, and I want to try it."

We were aware of the "Bob & Carol & Ted & Alice" movie about open marriage that came out in 1969, but had never watched it. I think the movie was too threatening for us, let alone what appeared to be happening on this warm Tuesday afternoon.

By now both of our glasses of ice cubes were clanking like marimbas. I was silent, trying to breathe.

"I don't want this to interfere with our marriage or our daily life, but I can see that this could be a good idea."

"What makes you think so?" I asked.

"Debbie took me out into the field and I guess you could say, seduced me. It was very exciting."

Ah, the dried grass aroma.

"She pulled Frank out there too, but he passed out from drinking too much. I had to almost carry him back to the house."

"What a bitch!" I said. "She shows up at my house, really never acknowledges my presence or says howdy-do—that pisses me off more than you were willing to be drug off into the bushes! Who does she think she is? And who are you? And where was her husband during all this time?"

"I don't know where he went, probably to his sleeping bag."

I should have thought to say he had drug me off to some other bushes and had his way. But, I was not very quick when I was upset.

"There's more," he said. "You saw her artwork. She wants to move down here and share a studio with me. We could make really great stuff."

"Oh swell!" I blurted out. "This is getting worse by the minute."

"Just calm down," he said, reaching for my knee with his right hand, which I batted away.

We sat for awhile, watching the ice melt in our shaking high-ball glasses.

"Are you sure you want to do this?" I asked.

"Yes, I am. It will be good for us, liven things up."

"Okay, then, I know this sounds trite, but what's good for the goose is good for the gander," I said, tossing my head back.

"What do you mean?"

"Just that. I will do an open marriage, too."

"With who?" he asked wide-eyed.

"I have no idea, but that's not your problem, is it?"

Some weeks passed. Carl made arrangements to meet the bitch somewhere for a weekend. I began chatting with the carpenter who was remodeling the beauty salon across the patio from the boutique. I wasn't flirting…I never learned how…but I did mention that my husband and I were experimenting with an open marriage. He looked both intrigued and a bit scared. He was studying to become a therapist of some sort, so he wasn't naïve about the ramifications of messing with a married woman. Or, her husband. Our conversations deepened, about the meaning of life and how to modify behaviors we weren't pleased with. I enjoyed his company, but that was it. Not much else could happen in a ten-by-fifteen foot glass house in the middle of a shopping center.

Carl went away on the weekends, and we survived it, always talking openly about our feelings and how this was all going. I didn't like the situation, but I had hope he would see the light.

He had met the carpenter and knew I was fond of him, but when I said, "It's my turn to have a weekend now," he blanched and then started sweating. No goose/gander for him. He stomped around for a bit. I just watched. And waited.

He said we should change the rules and not be away from home during normal hours…evenings and weekends…because of the kids. I honestly didn't want to go somewhere for a weekend, but I was interested in exacting some revenge.

"So, what are your new rules?"

"Well," he said, almost sheepishly. "We could meet our new friends for lunch. Or…for a nooner."

Where the heck would that take place?

But playing his game, and biding for time…*time heals all*…I told him I would cancel the weekend with the carpenter and reschedule a middle-of-the-week lunch. Or, nooner. He started sweating again, but acquiesced.

Over the next couple of weeks, Carl pursued several local women. They were initially drawn to him, as I was, but he told me later that once they met me, they decided they would rather have me for a friend than Carl for a lover. I was not feeling sorry for him.

The night before I was to go for the potential nooner, Carl turned into a ranting nutcase. He was pacing across the living room, back and forth, explaining all the reasons I should not go. I guessed the rules were changing again.

When he finally calmed a bit, he said, "Actually, this isn't working out like I thought it would. It's a lot of work."

I wanted to say, "I'm so sorry for you!" But, I held my tongue. I was relieved and had pretty much been sure it would work out this way. But I wasn't ready to totally agree.

"What about that woman coming down here and sharing a studio with you?" I asked.

"Well, I'd still like to do that. You can see the combination of my clay work and her graphic abilities. We could earn a lot of money with those pieces."

"Not an option," I said.

"What do you mean?" He actually seemed perplexed.

"Just what I said. She can't come here and you can't work with her. She's an unthinking, unkind bitch, and I don't want her anywhere in my greater aura, which includes yours, too."

I wasn't exactly sure how auras functioned, but it sounded good.

He finally calmed down enough to call Erik and Swen in from their early evening TV programs. We ate dinner, got them settled for the night and went to bed.

I certainly did not fall asleep, and I was pretty sure he was wide awake too, but I waited.

"You awake?" he whispered.

"Uh-huh," I responded.

He nudged my arm with his left hand and stuck his right arm straight up into the air, palm open and flattened, as if to shake.

"Okay," I said, quietly thrilled. "Remember it's your choice."

"I doubt I will ever forget," he said, taking hold of me.

In the morning, after Erik got on the bus and Swen was engaged with dominoes, I said, "I want you to write a letter to that woman, while I look over your shoulder, in which you tell her there are no more visits, no studio in the future. Nada. Zip. And then I will place it in the mailbox myself."

It may have seemed like I didn't trust him to accomplish this task, but I knew it was a difficult and hat-eating assignment. He wrote it. I mailed it.

We dropped Swen at nursery school and walked on the beach. Then we drove into Santa Monica and had lunch at the tallest restaurant in town, on Second Street. It was a gorgeous day. We could see from Point Dume to Palos Verdes.

Our lives returned to normal, if there was anything normal in those days, but I knew that woman would always be known to me as *the bitch from Utah*.

Encinal Canyon
1976

Encinal Canyon Road was cut into the Santa Monica Mountains with mostly sweeping curves and profusions of yellow Scotch broom. It was over four miles from the head of my driveway to the Pacific Coast Highway. I loved the freedom of not having to pedal, feeling the wind in my face and smelling the pungent broom blossoms.

On one bright day, I looped my long wrap-skirt into my waistband and set out for the colorful cruise down Encinal. While coasting around one of the tighter curves, my new, embossed leather journal flew out of the handlebar basket, passing my head like a wounded bird.

"Oh no," I groaned. I hit the brakes and skidded on some loose gravel, splatting onto the unforgiving asphalt. My lunch apples tumbled down the hill. My knees bled into my tights, and I could see the journal lying lonely and still in the middle of the road.

As I was ungracefully hoisting myself up, an old red truck rounded the bend. It swerved to miss my journal, and stopped next to me.

A young man, a boy really, looked at me and said, "Are you OK, Ma'am?"

My first thought was, *Ma'am? Do I look like a Ma'am already?* I was about thirty three to his eighteen.

My next thought was, *I've got to get my journal!*

"I'm fine. Thank you for asking. I'll just gather my stuff and be on my way," I said, brushing gravel off my hands and pulling my skirt down to cover my oozing knees.

"Are you sure? I could put your bike in my truck and take you where you were going."

"No, really, thank you so much," I repeated, gazing past him at my journal.

The young man's brow was wrinkled as he took a last look at me and finally drove off. My brow was probably wrinkled, too, about my journal. It was not that it contained any gritty gossip or deep inner thoughts. It was that it didn't.

I had been listening to Anaïs Nin read from her diaries on KPFK while working in the pottery studio. I was swept away by her stories of hanging out with Henry Miller, sipping red wine in Paris cafes and living on a houseboat. She shared her intimate conversations with her psychiatrist and her thoughts about her relationships.

My attempt at journaling thus far was reading like a calendar—where I went or who I talked to, rather than what I felt or discussed with my shrink or friends. It paled in light of Nin's adventures and conversations. Yet, I yearned to live in the deep intensity that she evoked in her writing.

I pulled my bike off to the side and trotted directly to the journal. My knees were burning and the palms of my hands ached.

Ahhh!

I clutched the journal to my chest and made my way back to the bike. I gathered my sprawled lunch bag and bruised apples. I put the journal at the bottom of the basket and used my sweater to secure its contents. The journey continued with less élan, more caution around the curves and a new resolve to live a life worth writing about.

Boy-San

1977

On a weekend in the spring of 1977 the phone rang.

"Hello?"

A voice new to me said tentatively, "Hello, this is Dee, Carl's first wife."

"Oh. Well, hi!" I had known of her existence since the first night Carl and I met, but had never seen her or talked to her. "I guess you would like to speak with Carl. I'll go get him."

"Yes, thank you."

I ran out to the shop and breathlessly hollered, "Dee's on the phone. She wants to talk to you."

When he came back into the house a half hour later, he summarized their conversation. "Carl Jr. is now seventeen and about to graduate from high school. His uncle has helped him get into Annapolis, and he wants to meet me before he goes away." Carl Jr. was two years old the last time his father had seen him.

"How do you feel?" I queried.

"Of course, I want to see him. But I feel nervous about it—like I'll be challenged that I abandoned him."

"You sorta did."

"Dee put my stuff out on the front porch. That's what ended it. And I was only seventeen or eighteen years old."

"But years passed. You could have called or written to him."

He glared at me. "You're not making this any easier."

"I'm sorry. Maybe this is an opportunity to clean it up." There were more glares.

He had reached out some years earlier when he was working on the oil rigs and earning a good income. He contacted Dee and told her he'd like to send some money for Carl Jr., who was around eight at that time. After asking how the boy was doing, he made a suggestion of a monthly amount. Dee said that would be fine. We sent money for a few months until Carl got laid off from the oil rig job. And that was that until the phone call in 1977.

"We made a plan for me to have lunch with Dee so I could catch up on Carl Jr.'s life up to now. Next week. In Orange County," Carl reported.

"I think this is a good thing," I nodded.

The day arrived. Carl changed his clothes at least three times, trying to look presentable for the lunch meeting. The wardrobe of this potter was somewhat limited. I could tell he was nervous by the way he was moving, quickly, back and forth to the mirror. There were sweat beads on his forehead, even though the weather was cool.

When he returned, he seemed relieved to have the process started of reconnecting with his first-born son. Carl and Dee chose a date for Carl Jr. to visit us. They decided he would drive to our pottery boutique and follow me home so he wouldn't get lost finding our dirt driveway in the mountains.

I was watching on the appointed date, somewhat nervously, for Carl Jr. to arrive at the boutique. I spotted him immediately. He was tall, over six feet and resembled his father, but with stunning coloring—bronze-hued skin, black hair and dark eyes. Dee was half Scottish, a quarter each Hawaiian and Chinese. The features from these countries combined with the Swedish genes of Carl Sr.'s father and the Northern European genes from his mother, had resulted in a creature with God-like looks.

I left the boutique and walked toward him.

"I guess you're Laura. This is Randy, my best friend. I asked him to come with me for moral support."

"Good idea," I replied, shaking their hands. "Do you want to take a look at your father's pottery while I close up the boutique?"

"Sure," they agreed.

The boutique was such a sweet place. How could he not appreciate the creative output of his father, especially when Dee had told Carl Sr. that Carl Jr. had been taking pottery classes, not knowing his father had become a potter.

After moving the pots that I had hung outside for the day into the boutique and locking the door, I pointed out my car. "Follow me."

We drove along Zuma Beach and continued on PCH until we turned right on Encinal Canyon. It was springtime and the blue ceanothus and yellow Scotch broom were in full bloom and fragrant—a nice introduction to our neighborhood.

I slowed as we approached our driveway and signaled we'd be turning left. We bounced down the rutted road and parked our cars between the two structures. I was imagining Carl Jr.'s and Randy's first impressions. While the landscaping was improving, the place was still not ready for *Better Homes & Gardens*.

I motioned for them to follow me toward the backside of the house, figuring the spectacular view would impress him more than the dwelling.

As we entered the living room, I watched Carl Jr. look up at the ceiling. There was no ceiling. It had advanced from the plywood roofing of the first couple of years, and was now covered with pink fluffy insulation. That was lined with silver foil, which might have appeared festive and sparkly were it not for name of the manufacturer stamped every few inches on the foil.

I saw Carl Jr. elbow Randy and lift his face toward the ceiling with a half-smile. His Orange County home probably had a normal ceiling.

Carl Sr. entered the living room from the front door, followed by Erik and Swen. They were now ten and six and had been told a brother they had never met was going to visit. The three boys looked at each other. The air was electric and the feeling tone was awkward.

I intervened. "This is Randy, Carl's best friend." The spell was broken and they all started smiling. I introduced Erik and Swen.

"Welcome," said the dad to the son he hadn't seen for fifteen years. The young men nodded but there was no hand shaking or hugging.

I intervened again. "I'm going to start fixing dinner." It was only four in the afternoon, but I didn't know what else to do.

Carl Sr. asked, "Would you like to come out to the studio?"

"Okay," and the five of them filed out the front door.

I plopped in a chair. Phew. I'd always been so close to my parents, and still was. I couldn't imagine what it would feel like to have not seen them since I was two, nor could I imagine not seeing Erik and Swen for fifteen years.

The evening went well, considering, with stories shared and no recriminations, like "Why didn't you stay in touch with me?" or "How come you abandoned me?" The young men left for home around ten.

The next sighting of Carl Jr. was when we were invited to his high school graduation. Once again, the four of us tried to figure out what to wear so we wouldn't look like country bumpkins. The party after the ceremony was in Dee's home, which she shared with her husband, Al. They were both very kind to us. The house had vaulted ceilings—no insulation in sight. Dee was as gorgeous as Carl Sr. had described her, with thick black hair and dark eyes and perfect features. She welcomed us, and we enjoyed the festivities. At least I did.

Carl Jr. decided Annapolis was too far away and enrolled at Cal Poly, San Luis Obispo. He spent weekends with us at least once a month, and we all got to know each other better.

The Carl Jr. and Carl Sr. thing became irritating. We tried Little Carl and Big Carl, but they were both big. Old Carl and Young Carl didn't sit well with the elder.

They became known as Papa-San and Boy-San.

Holistic Health

1978 and on...

My connection with New Age ideas started with my neighbor Pola, was amplified by Toni, the yoga instructor, and cemented by Gale, who was my first friend who was a devotee of Yogananda, one of the first East Indian gurus who came to the West. She was also a vegetarian at the time.

Ruthann, who was right alongside me in these pursuits, and I both subscribed to *New Age* magazine. It was filled with mind-expanding articles about people who were exploring spiritual lives different from those than they had grown up with, including new food ideas and the concept of holistic health.

Ever since Toni had exposed me to the ways in which yoga promoted good health, I was doubting the Western medicine that I had been trained in at nursing school and also curious about what else was available to study about health and healing.

I received a flyer for a holistic health conference in San Diego.

"Let's go!" I said to Gale, even though I was not accustomed to going out into the big world without Carl.

"It might not even happen since most people don't know what holistic health is. But I'm game for registering for it," I noted, thinking we were in the vanguard in this arena.

After insuring the conference would indeed go forward, and making arrangements with our families to be away for a long weekend, we set out for San Diego. We stopped at Encinitas where Yogananda had a hermitage and strolled in the beautiful gardens.

Not only was the conference a go, there were about 2,000 people present! What did we know in our isolated town?

It was my first exposure to Elizabeth Kübler-Ross. I wept throughout her entire presentation—the tiny Swiss-American psychiatrist who understood the importance of accepting death and being with the dying in a compassionate way.

I almost fell off my chair when an enormous gong was hammered—the sound went through my body in a way nothing else ever had.

A "recovering" Baptist minister talked about his "dark night of the soul" following a divorce and a bout of drinking. When he came out of it, his religious views had expanded to include all spiritual paths, and he no longer led his Baptist flock.

Another speaker described the alchemists and how their health practice included stopping eating before you were full, exercising and meditating. Gale already meditated regularly, but I was still at the twenty-minutes-per-week meditation at yoga class.

At the end of the weekend, I was so inspired and flustered.

What would all this would mean to me and the rest of my life?

One morning, upon awakening, Carl told me he'd listened to a fascinating program on the radio station KPFK. "They interviewed these African pygmies," he began. "They determine each other's health and what kind of treatments they need by examining deep lines in their elbows. They call it elbow mapping."

"Really?" I exclaimed, believing every word. Carl had figured out places where I was most gullible.

I called Ruthann to tell her this important news before I figured out he was teasing me.

From then on, all of our close friends and children referred to all New Age discussions as "elbow mapping."

Sometime during those years, I drove to Phoenix, Arizona, with my pal Dona, for a four-day conference at A.E.D., the *Association for Enlightenment and Development*. It was the closest West Coast place where Edgar Cayce's ideas were being taught. Cayce was a former shoe salesman and photographer who developed enormous psychic abilities following a severe sore throat. When he met with clients, he was able to diagnose their ailments and make suggestions of how to treat them. His wife and secretary wrote down all of these conversation, and they were then catalogued at the A.E.D. for anyone to use.

At the conference, in addition to stimulating lectures about Edgar Cayce himself, there were many topics presented that related to health and healing. There were great meals, singing and dancing, and a final dinner party when participants were asked to dress up as a character from a past life.

Ah, there was that reincarnation concept again.

I had no idea who I had been, so I didn't dress up. But it was a lot of fun looking at the folks who did wear costumes.

On the way home we had a flat tire, in the middle of the Arizona desert, at night. I was driving my very small Fiat. I got the instruction book out and Dona held the flashlight and read it while I unscrewed the lug bolts and lifted off the very small tire.

Success.

Oh, no! The spare was flat!

We stood at the edge of the wide, divided highway and determined the town we had just passed through was closer than the one we were approaching, although we didn't know for sure. So, I picked up the tiny tire and we schlepped across the desert-like median—it was deep, like traversing a canyon and then a mountain. That could be an exaggeration. Now we waited for approaching cars on the opposite side. When one was near, we started hopping up and down, waving our arms like mad women. No one stopped.

I said, "Dona, we've just been immersed in spiritual everything for four days. We are not doing this right." We decided to start singing, making up the words as we thought them up, something like, "It would be so lovely if you stopped and helped us with our flat tire, la la la la."

The very next car stopped. A nice man happened to have a can of tire-foam. Once sprayed into the tire, it would patch the hole. He did so, and voila! a new tire. We thanked him profusely. He wouldn't accept any money and told us his mother taught him to always help women in need.

We stumbled across the divider again, put the tire back on and set off for Needles, a small town near the border of California. We turned into the Mobil gas station, the one we had stopped at on our way to Phoenix and learned the station had been robbed at gunpoint thirty minutes earlier! We got a severe case of the giggles, believing wholeheartedly that angelic forces had gotten us there after the robbery took place.

Weeks passed while I absorbed the information and atmosphere of the people at A.R.E.

These conferences and seeing Elizabeth Kübler-Ross again stimulated Gale and me to pass on some of the information we had learned. We talked to Diane and Eileen, therapist friends of ours, and decided together to create a daylong retreat for women. It was, of course, called the Blue Sky Retreat for Women. I opened the day with yoga. Gale was already giving acupressure treatments. She partnered the guests and taught them simple and valuable treatment patterns.

After a sumptuous luncheon of my great whole wheat-berry bread and a large salad, Diane led the group in Assertive Caring. She had been teaching Assertiveness Training at UCLA and adapted its principles to providing self-care.

After coffee and cookies, Eileen led the participants in journal writing, based on Ira Progoff's book, *At a Journal Workshop*.

The day was clearly a success per responses from the guests. We hosted six to eight retreats over several years. Our husbands were less enthusiastic when we reported that after dividing the twenty dollar fees and subtracting expenses, we each earned about eighteen dollars per retreat. But it seemed worth it to us.

Personal Fire

1978

My kooky friend, Cheryl, had just given me a Tarot card reading at the boutique. The Tower had shown up in my fourth house of home, past and roots.

"What do you think that means?" Cheryl asked.

"I dunno. My parents are in good shape. Things seem good at home."

At that moment, a car pulled up to the boutique where there were no legal parking spaces. Two ladies leapt out of the car, one from each front door. I recognized them as the new occupants of the chalet up our driveway on the Knob. They ran toward me saying, "Fire! Fire! There's a fire!"

I stood up. "Where?" When there was a wildfire, everyone was on alert and passed on the word.

Just then, Carl pulled up, screeching brakes, with Erik and Swen. He saw the neighbor ladies and realized they must have witnessed the flames from their perch above us.

"We knew you didn't have a phone here so we thought we should tell you," one of them said.

Carl came into the boutique. "The studio caught on fire. It's gone."

Gone where? The studio, our old house, which now held our livelihood, was burned down?

My heart started pounding.

Carl went on, "I was eating lunch and smelled smoke. I looked out the front door and could see the flames. I ran barefoot across the field with a tortilla hanging out of my mouth. The firemen arrived right away and were next to the studio in minutes. But it was too late."

"Where was Swen?" I asked. Ever since he had learned to strike a match, he thought fire was the best toy ever. Despite our hiding matchbooks, we found him gleefully playing with fire now and then. In the winter, he tossed bits of wood into a burning fire in the fireplace or ran his little fingers through a candle flame, probably something Carl or Erik taught him.

"He was taking a nap, sound asleep."

I was relieved.

"The only thing I can think of," Carl went on, "is that maybe the surfer guys living in the trailer behind the studio left some rags with surfer wax lying around. Maybe tossed a cigarette. But they weren't even home. The firemen said it could have smoldered for awhile."

"How's the trailer?" I asked.

"Too damaged for them to live in."

"What do we do now?" I asked, slumping into my chair.

"The firemen want us to sleep somewhere else tonight while they keep an eye on the propane tank. It's right next to the hot remains of the building. They think it could explode."

We piled into the car and drove to Michael and Ruthann's. After we told the story and they fed us dinner, we arranged blankets on the floor of a spare room and tried to sleep. Not such an easy task.

"Oh, my God! Our bicycles!" I sat up and pictured them hanging from the rafters. Mine was one of the few things I had ever bought on my own, without anyone's permission.

Trying again to sleep, I sat up. "Oh, my God, the Miraculous Mutha's!" These were porcelain pipes with the creature from *Easy Rider* magazine, owned by my friend Carolyn's husband, Lou. Since the boutique sales had slowed down, Carl had accepted a few mass production assignments. He sculpted the form, made latex molds and poured porcelain slip into them. I was helping on weekends by smearing a brownish tint on them to amplify her ugly features. There were trays of her. Hundreds of her. Worth a lot of money to us. Same response when I remembered the Skull Mugs, also for *Easy Rider,* also ugly, but lucrative. Hundreds of those too, ready to be fired. They just weren't supposed to be fired by the building burning down.

Somehow, the night passed. We thanked the Saphiers for their hospitality and drove through the mountains to the Knob. We checked in with the firemen. They felt it was now safe for us to return home.

We called the landlords to tell them what happened. They listened and said they would call us back.

Mr. Griffin said, "Well, I have an insurance policy on that building for $16,000. If you can build something for that, you can have it."

We were shocked, thrilled—we didn't know what to think. Over the ten years we had lived there, the Griffins stopped by for a visit, maybe once a year, or to get something out of their storage. They had left belongings in the west module, now our bedroom. We had moved their things into a large red storage unit that Tom brought home from the airport, where he worked. The Griffins said they could see we had made this a home for ourselves and that maybe they would not return to live there when they retired, after all.

Wildfire

1978

It was a blustery day in October, 1978. Everyone was on pins and needles in the autumn months in Malibu. The season came with Santa Ana winds, which fueled wildfires and blew hot toward the ocean.

We were just getting back to a normal life after our "personal fire." There was smoke in the air but no one knew yet where it was. Someone ran into the boutique, saying, "There's a fire somewhere around Mulholland, not sure where." Mulholland stretched from downtown Los Angeles to the ocean. Parts of it were within a mile of the Knob.

Erik had stayed home with a sore throat. Swen was almost six now and at school. I closed the boutique and picked him up. We drove home, the air getting darker. Carl and Erik were already hosing down the buildings. Erik was ten by now and seemed game to help Carl, despite the sore throat. Tom was at his house doing the same.

Carl shouted, "You and Swen get back down the hill but go north toward Oxnard, because we can see flames already to the south of here."

I got our toothbrushes and a few clothes. On the way down Encinal, there were flames on both sides of the road, roaring through Charmlee Park. When I got to PCH, I could not imagine spending the night in Oxnard, where I knew no one. I turned south and drove to Diane's on Point Dume. The sky was almost black.

Diane showed us where we could put our belongings and sleep. We had some dinner together. Her husband Mike went out on his motorcycle every once in a while to see what he could find out. He saw eucalyptus trees burning close to the highway.

Swen slept through the night. I stayed awake. It was so difficult not knowing what was happening, or if we would have a home by the morning. When we got up in the morning, we found the fire had been controlled, mainly because it jumped the highway and burned homes right on the beach. The flames were stopped by the ocean.

I left Swen with Diane and drove home. No one was there, but the house was standing. The hills were black in every direction. The screens on the screen porch were melted. I drove back up the driveway to Tom's. He was sound asleep, sitting upright on his living room couch. I was so happy to see him, I leapt onto his lap and threw my arms around his neck. He later referred to this moment as the time I lap-danced with him, but that was far from my mind.

"Are you okay? Where's Carl and Erik?"

"I think they went looking for you and Swen," he groggily replied.

I ran back to my car and was on PCH between Encinal and Trancas when I saw Carl and Erik heading north. They saw me too, and Carl made an illegal U-turn. I pulled over. We all jumped out of our cars and hugged and cried. We were both tense and exhausted for different reasons—me from wondering what was happening, them from being in the midst of it all for most of the day and night.

I drove back to Diane's and picked up Swen and some food and went home where I heard their war stories.

Erik said, "When the flames got close, and it was blowing like crazy, we crawled under the dining room table until it passed over the house. Then we went out and poured water on the flames that were here and there on weeds or bits of wood."

I could see the paint on the outside of the house was bubbled.

Erik continued, "Mom, you just wouldn't believe how it was burning all around us and then it moved on down the canyon toward the beach." We had read about the firestorms doing just that and we were all glad we knew to wait it out.

"A fire engine parked on the fire road," Carl reported. It had been cut into the hillside from Encinal just below the four houses on the Knob. "They came up and told us they were watching our buildings. That took some of the pressure off."

Carl went on, "We made a plan with Tom late at night that we would take turns sleeping and watching for flames bursting out of hotspots. Erik fell asleep on the couch during his watch, but Tom saw a streak of flames coming straight toward our house. He jumped in his truck and roared down, waking us up. We poured buckets that we had filled on the flames. That was extra scary!"

I was really glad I didn't know about it as it happened. I was so relieved to be with my family. We made some breakfast and slept much of the day.

Looking out at the landscape was depressing. It was black as far as we could see. By the following spring, the hills were green again, though with black sticks of remaining chaparral poking up. Just as predicted, more wildflowers bloomed than ever—something about certain seed pods needing fire to open.

Paddle Cats

1978 - 1982

In the spring of 1979, our neighbors Eino, the Finnish marble sculptor, and his wife Krista, a German weaver, invited Carl to go kayaking past the point to see the migrating whales.

"It was exhilarating!" Carl exclaimed when he came home. "We were so close to the whales, almost at eye level. They just looked at us and continued on their way. I want to do that again and take you out there." It sounded good to me. I had always enjoyed seeing the whales from the coast highway, but up close sounded even better.

"But," Carl continued, "the kayaks are too little for me and too unstable. I was always feeling I was about to tip. I'm going to think of something better so we can do this more easily."

Uh, oh. Another complicated project. Can't he take up watercolors instead of needing to build kilns, throwing wheels or renting cranes to lift giant chunks of wood?

Little did I know what was coming next.

"I see a catamaran that is narrow enough to paddle, but stable enough to not tip over. There could be places for fishing or scuba gear. We could sleep on the canvas netting if we went camping."

The excitement was contagious, despite what I feared would follow.

We knew a marine engineer who became excited when Carl described his idea. He drew up some designs, getting the appropriate length and width. Then Carl started welding giant machines which were used to press polyvinyl chloride sheets into the shapes of half-hulls, and were then glued together. A frame was created to tie the two hulls together. He found a seamstress to hem the mesh fabric that would serve as a deck. A few pairs of paddles were procured. Voila! A Paddle Cat! Carl, Erik and Swen took turns paddling it a bit forward and back in our Doughboy pool. They were quick trips, since the pool was only sixteen feet in diameter.

Carl created places to hang and tie down the paddles, fishing poles and scuba tanks. A few more Paddlecats were built and we tested them in the ocean. The boats plowed through the surf, remained level to the sea, and were fun as could be. Paddling so close to the surface of the water, I could see rows of sand dollars on the floor of the ocean at Zuma Beach.

We started advertising. Fishermen Carl knew bought the first few. They were tired of having to gas their small boats up and launch them off of a pier. My friend Susan bought one and took it up to Decker Lake where she lazily floated and cast out her artistic, tied flies.

Carl was thrilled. The bad news was, he wanted to close the boutique. Business had slowed down somewhat the previous year or two. We figured it was because most Malibu residents had at least one of every item we sold. At times, we thought an earthquake might spur business if enough pottery was broken. But Carl said he really could not make another wine goblet or coffee mug, our most popular items.

I was heartbroken to imagine leaving the boutique, but I didn't want to keep it to sell just any old merchandise. I liked our total family involvement. But I placed ads to sell the remaining pottery, plants and cards. We sold almost everything including the hanging racks, except for two we took home, one for the kitchen, and one for the front porch. A Malibu family, who had been selling flowers next to the boutique, took it over. I was informed by the plaza manager that I didn't have a business to sell. Since she had only charged us one hundred fifty dollars per month over five years, I figured we were even. I said a temporary farewell to the plaza and Lily's bakery, where I got my daily cream cheese delight so easily, and said goodbye to the plethora of delicious stories and chats. I returned to the mountain and started helping with the bookkeeping and advertising of the Paddle Cats.

As I began answering the requests from prospective customers, showing them how easy it was to get a Paddle Cat off the top of a car, carry it to the water and, providing it was not stormy, paddle it through the surf, I developed some hidden strength and bravery. It was exhilarating and another chapter of life opened.

Catalina

A highlight of those years was Paddle Catting Catalina! Our fisherman friend, Wayne, took five of us and five Paddle Cats on his fishing boat to the west end of Catalina. Over three days, we paddled from there to Avalon. In the evening, we pulled into sheltered coves and beached the boats. Carl and Rick went scuba diving and brought back lobster and fish for dinner. We slept on the fabric decks out in the open in the sandy coves. Stars were plentiful.

In the early mornings after coffee, homemade bread and jam, we pushed out into the glassy, flat ocean. Looking down into the water, we could see golden garibaldi swimming among the rocks. If we looked up, there were mountain goats cavorting on the very steep cliffs, never losing their foothold.

We stopped at the Isthmus, a low place between the western and eastern portion of the island. We had lunch and Mai Tais at a cafe with palm-branch palapas. It became known as Mai Tai Heaven during future Catalina trips.

Each day was filled with new wonders and vistas and meals. It was perhaps the best vacation I ever had. On the fourth day, we pulled into the harbor at Avalon, the main town of Catalina. It was bustling and colorful. We stored the Cats near the ferry landing while we had lunch and explored the harbor sites. It was fun to see the tiled walls along the promenade, the backdrop in photos of my parents on their honeymoon in 1935. Not too much had changed except for more cafes and hotels.

The ferry took us to San Pedro where we had left a car. Somehow, Carl tied all five Cats on top of our Chevy "floater"—one of those long sturdy cars from the late sixties, a gift from Michael and Ruthann. We were sad when Avalon slipped out of view, but we could still see the mountains of Catalina, only "26 miles Across the Sea."

New Friends

Carl's diving buddy, Bob, had a friend who lived on the bluff near Decker Canyon. They were able to carry the Paddle Cats down the cliff to a beach with a beautiful reef, filled with lobsters and abalone. Carl noticed a shack part way down the bluff and asked what it was for. A deal was made: we could use the shack to store the Cats in exchange for the owner to use them. It turned out the inside was decorate-able—I made it into a sea shanty and we slept there on some weekends.

On the beach below, we met a new family, John and Wendy Powell, who also had two sons. Christian and Jesse were younger than Erik and Swen, but they all had fun together playing in the surf and sand. John and Carl became fishing buddies, and Wendy and I shared our life stories as we watched the boys play. In the evenings, we shared grilled seafood. Years later, they helped us buy our house.

The Young Investor

About a year or two into this adventure, a youngish man approached us at the beach and asked if he could take a Paddle Cat out. "I've been watching you, and I'm intrigued."

"Sure," I said, thinking of a potential sale.

His name was Peter, and it turned out that he was a trust-funder. He expressed an interest in investing in the business. Since the regular income from the boutique had stopped, we were back to living from one boat sale to the next, and the word investment was pretty enticing. And, scary. It meant, to me, someone else running the show, lack of control and a daily life that was not the laid-back days we enjoyed.

And that's what happened. A corporation was formed. We had to get an accountant, and I had to do the monthly reports "to the penny." I was accustomed to "somewhere near the penny." We did receive a monthly salary for the two of us, which was quite dandy, but I still felt uneasy.

After some months passed, Peter suggested we make a wider version of the Paddle Cat, which of course meant you couldn't paddle it. Carl had designed a sail for the Paddle Cat but it was not sea-worthy. Peter liked to sail and Peter had the money——but I could see the writing on the wall. The Wind Cat was born, and less interest was paid to the Paddle Cat.

Travel

Despite my concerns, the best thing that happened during the "time with

Peter" was travel. We applied to be in boat shows. Neither of us had seen much of the United States, and this venture allowed us to explore New Orleans and Chicago, two cities we might never have seen. And they were both worth putting up with Peter.

In New Orleans, we enjoyed beignets and chicory coffee in the morning and raw oysters and too much wine in the evening. Michael Saphier gave us one hundred dollars to go out for a special dinner, which we did at a converted pre-Civil War mansion on Lake Ponchartrain.

In Chicago, I walked along the lake in crystal clear weather. I had always pictured this city to be industrial and, therefore, full of smog and pollution. I didn't know the power of lake wind. We ate Greek food in one of the many different ethnic areas of the city.

The boat shows themselves were tedious and, aside from a few orders, not profitable. In the early spring of 1981, I could see Peter's interest waning, but was shocked when he left a message one morning saying he would no longer participate and no further funds would be deposited in our bank.

Uh, oh.

It was not only a big upset, but I had already paid bills planning on the amount of our monthly income being there to cover them. It wasn't. The manager of our local bank had been one of my patients at Dr. Hodges, and I was embarrassed. We had no money to cover the checks I had written. It finally got resolved by some slightly underhanded plan that included the idea that the bank should have known enough to check the deposit first. But I parked at the far end of the parking lot for many years to avoid seeing the bank manager who had covered for us.

The energy for the Paddle Cats waned when Peter backed out. So much work had been put into project and now it wasn't what it started out to be. The future vision was gone, too.

The Powells took our family to Maine where they had a summer cabin on Toddy Pond, very similar to Golden Pond, with loons calling out and fish jumping out of the water. We rested and swam and ate lobsters with big claws, different from Pacific Ocean lobsters. We returned refreshed.

John introduced Carl to a neighbor who was exploring raku pottery. Carl spent time with him and his enthusiasm for clay returned but in a very different form. He started building the kind of kilns needed to fire the pottery with smoke to make unusual glazes. He also started making very big pots, far larger than the coffee mug size.

The Powells and their friends, the Caplows, were well-connected to the Design Center in Los Angeles, affectionately known as the Blue Whale. They introduced Carl to a particular showroom that seemed like a good fit, and they agreed to represent him.

Our fortunes seemed to be changing once again.

The Seminal Weekend

1981

It was the long weekend following Thanksgiving of 1981. Our friends Barbara and Victor, Linda and Jim, and Bob and Judy all had the normal family dinners as usual on Thursday. Even though one family lived near San Diego and another north of San Francisco, we four couples ended up hanging out at our home for the rest of the weekend. Not everyone slept at our home, but we regrouped every morning after breakfast. There were hikes, hot tubbing, more food and lots of laughter.

Each of the couples included one successful creative person and one seemingly not creative person. There was Carl, the potter and sculptor, and me; Bob, the published writer, and Judy; Victor, the published writer, and Barbara; and Linda, the actress and dancer acclaimed on both coasts, and Jim. The non-creative spouses functioned as support members for the artists: the promotion, the paperwork, the listening to new ideas, not to mention keeping their households running. Among us there were six young children who cavorted happily throughout the house and yard during our gathering.

Something had been burbling up inside me for a long time, but I didn't know what it was or what to call it. So, maybe I instigated the huddle in the living room with the non-artists.

I shared that most recently Carl and I had been hosting pottery sales. Often I would hear someone say a version of, "Oh, you guys are so creative!" Without a moment's hesitation, I would respond, "Oh, not me. It's just him!" Or, someone might say, "I just can't draw a straight line." And I would follow with, "Me, neither." As if drawing a straight line was the true way of knowing a creative being.

So, here we were, the four "non-creative-in-the-world" spouses, gathered around the fireplace on a cold November afternoon. It was too early for wine so our conversation had a serious tone.

I asked, "What's the deal here? Why are *they* producing art and we are not? What is creativity? Were they born with it, and we were not? Or were they nurtured to develop it, and we were not? Is a product, such as a platter, a book or a part in a play the only measure of creativity? Why do we automatically help them with whatever they need—right now!"

I was on a roll. These questions oozed from the muck and mire that swirled unnamed in my psyche.

Each of us was thoughtful for awhile. Judy was raising her children, plus a special breed of dogs and said she didn't have time to think about being creative. Jim was interested in making videos, but nothing had come of it so far. Barbara had been immersed in the writing world, not only through her husband, but also via her father who was an editor at a large publishing house. She had worked there between college semesters but had never written herself. And me? I was the quintessential Virgo homemaker/gardener, keeping our home pretty—if not all that clean—but being a handmaiden for the great artiste! There were some vague responses to my queries, but they were more like stirring the pot than serving the meal.

The five years at the boutique had shown me I had a knack for making a welcoming space and for being with people. Hardly an hour passed that someone wasn't sitting in the chair across from me, telling me a story or their troubles. But once Carl moved onto the Paddle Cats and we closed the boutique, I was back on the mountain, weeding, making bread and asking how high when asked to jump. I had not considered that interaction with other people was a creative gift.

As we gathered around the long oak counter in the kitchen that evening to cut and chop leftovers into quesadilla fillings, we were quiet outwardly, but the conversation had not left my mind.

I thought about my mother who had loved art. She considered it her high school major. But The Depression of 1929 coincided with her graduation, and she was not able to go to art school. Her father told her she had to help support the family. Later in life she dabbled in oil painting, and the two of us even took some lessons from a starving painter in Venice Beach. He and his family were having onion sandwiches for dinner the first night we were there. I think he was glad for the income but probably not inspired by either of us. I didn't continue my introduction to visual art, but the imprint of these moments was part of the sifting and storage process for what came later. My mom found other classes at the Y and continued painting.

Our neighbor Pola had taught me to make square, gold-wire jewelry. I became proficient enough to sell it at the boutique, but I was pretty much copying what she taught me. I can't recall that I made my own original designs. I also made some porcelain picture frames while helping Carl in the studio. They sold at the boutique, but were kind of clumpy—the round openings not quite round, the rectangles often like squares or parallelograms. I was still looking for an art form, but I was definitely not a painter, potter or a jeweler.

Once the first version of the Paddle Cats was completed and selling, I had no problem hoisting one above my head and charging through the surf to demonstrate their simplicity and light weight to prospective clients. But that did not seem creative to me, just kind of gutsy.

After that seminal weekend, Barbara sent a watercolor of my front porch, framing a poem:

To let you know
We enjoyed your salon,
With writers and artists,
actors, and moms

Your home is enchanting
The food divine,
Not to mention the four
bottles of wine

The energy which flows
Through your front door and home
Is there, like your friends,
For reasons well known

So just to say thank you,
For letting us share,
Inspiring moments
With people who care

The poem and painting awakened me. I had an inkling that I did have something to say, though what or how, I had no idea. We had purchased a Smith-Corona typewriter so I could make invoices for the Paddle Cats and do the bookkeeping. So maybe it would become a tool for my endeavors.

I had no spot of my own—and I had read about the importance of that in Virginia Wolf's *A Room of One's Own*—another arrow in the target of my discontent. I cleared a stack of thirty-three rpm albums from a shelf in our closet—it was a multi-use room as it housed our turntable and record collection, as well as our shoes and humble assortment of clothes, including my seventeen long skirts and Carl's rugged work clothes.

There was the typewriter on the shelf, which I could use while standing up. I decided to start my first creative idea by interviewing Carlos, our friend from Chile, because his life, to me, had been so worldly. I knew nothing about interviewing, despite hours of listening to them on KPFK public radio while working in the studio.

Carlos was a willing subject and let me ask a series of questions I thought of. I returned to my closet-office and typed it up. I asked Carl, and Erik who was now around twelve or thirteen, if they would listen to me read my first piece of creative writing. They listened quietly. I finished. They remained quiet. One of them finally said something and I know it was not critical or mean. But I could hear my own words out loud—it was clumsy and uninformative, despite the unique character of Carlos.

I turned away without saying anything and went into our room. I threw myself on the bed and started sobbing.

Where, oh where, and how will I find my creative gifts? My voice?

It wasn't long before those questions began to be answered, but not in any way I had imagined.

Writing & Dancing
1982 – 2006

Two things happened as I pondered my thoughts on creativity after the seminal weekend.

First, my friend Chris called. "Did you know there is a dance-exercise class at the Malibu West Swim Club on Tuesdays and Thursdays from 5:30 to 6:30 called Maxi-Dance?"

She must have known I would be pleased with this news, so she spit it all out in one sentence. We both had children and husbands to tend to, so it was good news that the class was on our end of town, easier to get to.

I was excited, to say the least. I was a dancer at heart but had never trained after tap-dancing at age three came to an end because my mother said I wouldn't practice. I had loved the sound of the taps and the tutus that we wore.

This was the swim club where I had attended yoga classes, which was one of the first big changes of my life. It was like going home again.

"Carl, there is a new dance class at the Malibu West Swim Club. I am going to go to it."

"When is it?"

"5:30 to 6:30 on Tuesday and Thursday."

"What about dinner?"

I had expected this and was prepared. "I'll get dinner ready before I go, zip down the hill and be back up and we'll eat." It's not that I was a prisoner in my own home, but we had our routines. Since the end of the boutique years, I fixed the meals, ran the house, and he earned the money. At least he saw it that way. I was the backbone of his money-earning, from my point of view.

I could tell he wasn't thrilled, but I was.

The teacher's name was Maxine and a woman I knew named Bunty was her assistant. She did the bookwork and promotion. Kinda like I did at home. The dancing was loosely modeled on Jazzercise or Dance Aerobics in that it included repetitive steps to fun music. But Maxine had been a professional dancer, so the simple-to-learn moves had a definite dance-like flair. I was in heaven. I didn't realize how much I wanted to dance, and boy, I had those dinners figured out after breakfast on class days. It all worked. No fussing.

After a few months, Maxine and Bunty asked me to stay after class.

"Would you be interested in teaching the class at another location? We can see you're a good dancer and we're looking to expand."

I must have looked shocked.

I was being thrown into a briar patch! Me? Teach dance classes at age thirty-nine?

I gasped my answer. "Yes! I would like that. Very much."

"Good. Bunty will teach you the routines, and then when you're ready, we'll talk about where."

I practiced as if my life depended on it.

BLUE SKY BODYWORKS

Around the same time, my friend Barbara had been driving up and down the state of California securing permits and grants to turn an abandoned elementary school into a community center on Point Dume because of a decrease in population. She was a visionary; she couldn't bear the school and its grounds being unused and slowly decaying. I am sure a lot of the locals felt that way, but Barbara made it happen.

As she put the pieces together, I saw the perfect segue to where I would teach Maxi-Dance. The timing looked as if it would be perfect. Meanwhile, I loved going to the classes and learning how to teach them.

When I was deemed ready, and the community center was opened, I suggested to Maxine that I start teaching there. It was about four or five miles from the swim club. I believed it was far enough out of her range of competition.

Maxine said, "Oh no, you need to go to another town where you can gain experience."

"But I don't want to go to another town. This is where I live, where my people are." It wasn't like I wanted to open my own class in her same space.

She was adamant. While I was definitely growing and getting a mind of my own, and I was grateful to her for teaching me at no cost, I didn't want to step on her toes. So, I capitulated and said, "Okay, then. I'll teach yoga instead, because the community center is where I want to be. And I want to be part of it."

That wasn't good enough for Maxine. She said, "No you can't do that, because people know I have been training you, and it will reflect on me if the class isn't professional enough."

Barbara and Diane and I met for coffee and I told them about the drama unfolding.

Diane rolled her eyes and said, "Are you kidding? Who does she think she is? She doesn't even live in Malibu!"

Barbara chimed in. "I support you in whatever you want to teach at the center."

I ran with her encouragement and reported my plans to teach dance exercise at the community center to Maxine. She was surprised and not pleased. It was the beginning of me learning to take a stand—even if I still needed a lot of support.

Home School & Heartlight School
1982 – 1983

THE OREGANO CAPER

Erik was now in seventh grade. There had been an incident at a kid's birthday party where Erik and several others were caught poking holes in tires of neighborhood cars. A parent complained and the situation was handled between us, the boy instigator and the victims of the flat tires.

We discussed it all with Erik. He was recalcitrant, not arrogant, but still I could see he was becoming a teenager and trying to find a new place in his world. There were no teenagers on the mountain except Tasha, and she was going to a private Catholic school. It seemed like he was reaching for social acceptance, out of our close embrace.

Then the school called. "Will you please come in for a meeting? We need to talk about some recent activities."

We made the appointment and showed up, along with two or three other boys and their parents.

The story was that a girl reported being handed a film can of dark green, fragrant leaves. She then handed it off to Erik and another boy. A teacher spotted that interaction and called them all in. While neither Carl nor I used marijuana—we preferred wine and margaritas—it wasn't something that freaked us out. Many of our friends used marijuana. It was more about the disobeying of school rules that concerned us.

It was almost the end of the semester, and Erik and all the participants were suspended for the remaining days of the school year. We were adjusting to that news, when we got another call. "Please come in again," the principal said.

Now what?

We waited for the assembly of parents and students to gather.

"John's mother took the time and trouble to have the contents of the film can analyzed, because the student who initially had the film can reported he had found it in a campground. The report is that the contents were oregano, not marijuana."

"But if everyone believed it was marijuana, shouldn't the punishments be the same?" I asked.

"The school board says we have to move forward as if it were oregano." I didn't believe for a moment that it was oregano, but was not unhappy for Erik's record being cleaned up.

Then the school counselor asked me to come with her. She took me to Erik's locker.

"Look here," she said. She pointed to a couple of sticks connected by a short rope.

"What are they?" I had never seen such items.

"They are nunchucks. They're considered to be serious weapons and not allowed on the school's premises."

She stood there while I took in that bit of information so soon after the marijuana had been magically turned into oregano.

"I'm not going to report him, because I know he is a good kid. But you better do some serious talking with him."

I thanked her and felt relieved once again by Erik's reputation being saved by some sort of angel looking out for him. But I also felt as if it was serious enough to consider what we should do next. We had the summer to think about it.

Home School
Carl, Erik and I decided on home school. It wouldn't hurt to give Swen a break, we thought. I found places that provided teaching materials for homeschoolers, and we settled into a routine the following September. We met at the dining room table. I found a blackboard to sit on the old piano and I spread out the books and study plans in front of us. We managed to be this formal two or three times a week, but it wasn't easy without the structure of a regular school.

At the time, a Frenchman named Rene was living in the studio helping Carl. We asked him if he'd like to teach a bit of French.

"*Mais oui,*" he said. "May I have a piece of chalk?"

The first thing he wrote on the blackboard was, "*Mange mon bete.*" It turned out to translate as, "Eat my dick!" The boys loved this sacrilege and laughed and laughed as they repeated the phrase to taunt each other.

I planned field trips. One day, we picked up my mom and drove to Highland Park so they could see the house and neighborhood where I lived when I was their age. Then we went to Watts Towers. I had always been drawn to these mosaic-covered towers, built over decades by an Italian immigrant. I had read about them and the fundraising efforts to preserve them when city officials considered tearing them down, but I had never seen them myself. I was doing my own homeschooling.

Despite the fact that the towers were covered with scaffolding, we were all impressed with their height, the number of them and the colorful mosaics and mirrors attached, all created by one man and his vision.

Aunt Helen, my mother's younger sister, lived nearby. She was surely worthy of a field-trip stop. She was expecting us and had prepared lunch.

I noticed a small wooden frame of a picture of Jesus. "Aunt Helen, I have the same frame and picture of Jesus, too!"

"Yes, they were made by Mr. Watson before he died. He gave them to everyone he met."

I missed the historical context, but as she returned to the kitchen the boys and my mom were trying hard to keep from laughing. "What?" I said. Erik responded, "Mom, he couldn't have made them after He died!" I saw the cause of their glee and tried to shush them.

Helen returned to the living room with hors d'oeuvres. On a tray were four paper medicine cups containing a bright green substance that barely resembled an avocado in color. "This is guacamole," she informed us. Next to each cup were three small-sized Fritos. My aunt had been unusual since her premature birth, but her generous spirit surpassed all my other relatives. I knew how pleased she was to be serving a meal to us. As she returned to the kitchen to cook the main course, my family was definitely having the giggles, despite my trying to contain them.

Then we heard Helen say in the kitchen, "Oh shit!" That put them over the edge. She was hardly a person to cuss, but there it was, out of context.

Finally, she served stir-fried Chinese vegetables, no small feat, and three M&M's per person for dessert. I felt so touched by her efforts and didn't know whether to laugh or cry.

Heartlight

Now that Ruthann's second child, Adam, was school age, Ruthann had begun teaching at a small, private school called Heartlight. The first year, they met at the director Jack Zimmerman's home in Calabasas.

I didn't believe we could afford it, but Ruthann and Jack invited us to join them when we could or when there were special events. During that year, we went downtown with them to see "Fiddler on the Roof" at the Music Center. The school of about twenty-five kids aged five to seventeen came to our home twice for clay workshops that Carl presented. Jack also included Erik and Swen on a weeklong trip to the Ojai Foundation, where they camped, hiked and spent quiet time alone.

The following year, we were invited to attend Heartlight School, which had moved to an old complex in Canoga Park. Carl agreed to continue with art classes. I offered to teach anatomy and physiology every Friday, and I painted some of the buildings as needed, to trade for tuition.

Each school day began with a council, sitting in a circle and passing a talking stick. Some days the topic would be highs and lows of the preceding day. The students could share dreams or experiences that had been meaningful. Only the person holding the talking stick could speak, while all the others focused on that one person. It was the beginning of a helpful way of communicating in our family.

The boys returned to the Ojai Foundation again for the weeklong vision quest. We met Sue Robin, the administrator and her son Seth. I already knew Sandra and her son Chris from Ruthann's neighborhood. Patsy and Frank enrolled their son, Teddy. Our friendships deepened and remained. There was nothing superficial about Heartlight.

Kenny Loggins was a friend of Jack's. He asked the children what they liked about the school. David Saphier said, "I like the love," which became the first line of a song Kenny wrote, called "Heartlight!"

One day a kid named Chris punched Erik hard enough to knock him over. I was furious and ready to ask Jack to expel the boy after Erik told me about the incident.

The phone rang. It was Jack. "Chris would like to speak to Erik. Would Erik be willing to talk to him?"

Erik took the phone. He reported that Chris apologized and said he was angry about something related to his family, and Erik was the first person he ran into. Erik accepted his apology and we went on. Incidents like this made me happy that we'd able to have this enriching experience.

In the spring, Erik said he wanted to return to his old junior high so he could graduate from the ninth grade. We agreed.

Swen jumped off a low wall and broke his arm during the lunch hour on one of my teaching days. I called Carl and asked him to meet me at Dr. Hodges' office. He asked if I minded if I went without him. It was a good choice. After giving Swen a Demerol injection, the doctor had me sit on the examining table, legs apart, with Swen in front of me, my arms wrapped around his torso. He took hold of the broken arm. "Hold tight," he said. I did. He pulled, hard, until we heard the familiar sound of the bone falling back into place. Despite the Demerol, Swen wailed, until the moment the bone was in alignment again. Carl would have been green in color for sure.

Swen finished the year at Heartlight. When he returned to his elementary school for the fifth grade, his math and reading skills seemed to have receded. I took him to a tutor who was appalled we had let him slip behind the normal learning curve. She helped him a great deal. I let her know all of his accomplishments in the future, especially when he graduated from UCLA. He had a great fifth grade year with a wonderful teacher, Mr. Benbrook. The once-shy Swen organized a limo ride for him to the year-end festivities. While Swen's book skills may have suffered at Heartlight, both sons gained something more important that continues to be reflected in their adult personalities: a kindness, a willingness to listen and an interest in other people's stories.

The Undertoad

1983 - 1984

At first, the change from selling giant urns instead of coffee mugs seemed fortunate. We were able to buy some city clothes to wear to the Design Center. We met interesting new people, especially Sibyl and Al. Sibyl painted floral and abstract designs onto fabric, creating beautiful quilts and pillows. They were other "artist-types" at the Blue Whale amidst the designers and salesforce. During long weekend shows, we were able to hang out together and get to know them. We visited them in San Diego.

Restaurant dinners with upscale new acquaintances occurred with increasing frequency. At first, I was delighted to eat out, but then it began to feel like too much...or decadent. We were having fewer dinners with our sons. Even though our income had increased, it felt wasteful to spend so much money on food. If I complained, Carl snapped at me. "We're lucky to have these experiences! Just try to enjoy something new."

He was partially right. I had never been comfortable with change, but I could feel the stability of our family fraying at the edges. Plus, something was wrong with my innards. What had been a pang at the time of ovulation was now a severe pain for about two weeks, every other month. A friend of ours was a radiologist and arranged for me to have an ultrasound at his hospital. Despite our newfound wealth, we hadn't yet applied for health insurance. The test revealed material wrapped around my ovaries and fallopian tubes. The physical pain increased in my belly, as well as my angst about something being not quite right externally.

We got health insurance. I filled in the blanks about my pain and ultrasound, indicating something was wrong. The insurance agent missed that information and okayed coverage for a hysterectomy, which should have not occurred; it was a pre-existing condition. We were grateful to have eighty per-cent of the costs paid.

As I recuperated from the surgery, my girlfriends came up to the Knob with delicious lunches. We sat in the patio and talked about our lives as we approached forty. I could picture a new future, free from abdominal pain, teaching my dance exercise classes and worrying less about finances.

Carl went to Costa Rica with his new pottery friend. He returned a changed person, talking about renewal, inspiration and growth. I felt the same as I did when he started creating the huge wood sculptures—impressed and fearful. The weeks and months continued with decreasing degrees of normalcy, until nothing seemed normal.

The Mistaki Club

1984

We had breakfast and had got the boys onto the school bus. Carl walked out the front door, across the yard to his studio.

He hollered back, "Come out when you can. We need to talk."

Since we both worked at home, and talked all the time, it seemed an odd request. But the recent months had been different. After returning from Costa Rica early, Carl had seemed anxious, was drinking more, leaving the Knob more often than usual, and not saying where he was going or what he was doing. If I asked, he replied vaguely, "I'm sort of on a vision quest." He was also wearing very nice clothes when he wasn't working that made him look extra handsome, but unfamiliar.

I was the vision quest person in our family—going to conferences of New Age speakers, doing yoga and reading every last book of various spiritual teachers.

He often teased me about this, yet did not dissuade me.

My friend Sandra had invited me to work in her new Art and Craft Gallery in Ocean Park one day a week. I accepted at once. She was even going to pay me twenty dollars.

We were driving past Pepperdine University when I told him of this new opportunity for me to be in the midst of art, help Sandra, and maybe have lunch at a trendy restaurant.

"I don't want you to do that," Carl said. "I want you to be home so you can make lunch."

"But I don't want to make lunch 365 days a year!" I yelled.

This was the new me claiming another piece of myself.

I could feel there was something changing with both of us but it was still beneath the surface.

"Are you having an affair, or what?" I'd asked a couple of times. "No," he replied with some emphasis. We'd been through some rough patches before, but he was always honest, even if he behaved badly, so I accepted his answers.

I washed up the dishes and strolled over to the studio. As part of his new journey, he had created a sitting area in one corner of the studio. He had begun going out there after dinner a few nights a week.

He was in his early forties. Could be going through a midlife crisis? But didn't we already do that with the open marriage attempt?

I sat down in a stuffed chair. Clay dust poofed into the air. The neon sign across from me was missing the cross bars on the E. It read: THE MISTAKI CLUB. We'd chuckled about how that sounded for years: it was perfect with the mismatched lumpy chairs—as in more than a mistake.

The Santa Ana winds were blowing through the cracks in the sliding doors. A crackling energy permeated the dusty air. I thought about wildfires that often were caused by and fueled by the Santa Anas. It was difficult to sleep in our cliffside house during the winds—the building felt unstable, and the ominous sounds kept us on guard, waiting.

It was autumn and a few months from our twentieth anniversary. We had already had a few conversations about how we might celebrate.

Maybe he wants to firm that up?

I waited for him.

"Hey," he said as he sat down. I looked across the splintery coffee table at his blue eyes and red beard. His hair was tied back with a bandana. He usually had an impish smile that always warmed my heart. But he wasn't smiling.

He squirmed a bit, settling into the chair and looked around the studio without making eye contact.

Uh, oh, This does not feel like anniversary party chat.

"So...what's up?"

"I've met someone," he said quietly, not looking at me.

I felt the air exit my lungs. If I'd stood up I wasn't sure if my knees would have held me. It wasn't that there hadn't been other betrayals in the twenty years. He was a handsome guy and was often pursued by other women. Occasionally, he had difficulty saying no. But this felt serious. Neither of us talked for a while.

"Who?" I finally uttered.

"Can't tell you."

"Why? Is it someone we know?"

"Not saying."

"Is it Ursula?" I asked. Her name popped into my head for no reason. I knew I was trying to grasp at something concrete, something that I could alter if only I had more information.

"Was there a woman in Costa Rica?"

"Yes, but that was just a part of it. And that's not the woman I'm talking about. I had started feeling old, like I was doing the same thing day after day. And suddenly, I felt young again and energetic."

Oh, God. This sounds like a magazine article! How can he be so trite? He's different than other men! How could he can sound so much like a middle-aged man in a sitcom?

He went on, "When I got back from Costa Rica, I thought I would explore a bit and try to hold onto that feeling. It wasn't just about women or sex. I started swimming and snorkeling in the ocean again. I practiced not telling you everything on my mind as I always had. Just some kind of opening to a missing part of me."

I nodded. I wasn't crying, maybe because I was in shock. But I was shaking.

"So, I didn't expect to meet someone that would cause an upheaval in our family, our life. But it just feels too big."

Crimeny. Another TV line.

"Bigger than both of us?"

By now, I was getting mad. He was starting to earn good money with the big raku pots. We had bought our house a year earlier, after renting month-to-month for sixteen years. I saw the Tower card from the Tarot deck crashing, everything falling apart. I was not good at expressing anger but something was sure brewing up a storm in my guts and my armpits. I was sweating and shaking.

"Well." I stood up. "Well!" I said louder, but still couldn't come up with something pithy and punishing. Then, I did. "If you are going to mess around, then I will too!" I was trying to avoid, 'What's good for the goose is good for the gander,' so I wouldn't sound like a sitcom myself.

He didn't like this picture, I could tell. We'd been there before.

"But you've got the boys to take care of, and, maybe this won't last. Just give me a chance to explore it."

"Fine! Explore all you want. I will, too!"

I wasn't expecting capitulation, but I wanted to cause the same discomfort that I was feeling. Before I stomped out of the studio, I turned to look back at Carl. He was leaning forward with his hands on his head, his elbows on his knees. For a moment, I felt for him and the conflagration he had initiated. But then there was a flicker of freedom and a different life flashed before me.

Maybe the winds of a vision quest were blowing my way too, despite the anxiety that was surfacing.

The Santa Anas never blew again without my recalling the tension and sorrow I felt in the Mistaki Club that day.

Living on The Knob as Carl's Neighbor

1986 - 1999

Tom to the Rescue

1984

We tried to live a normal life for the next week or so, but there was nothing normal about anything. Family dinners were painful. Erik had just turned sixteen and Swen was almost twelve.

How were we, or rather how was I, going to make it through the teen years with this upheaval?

"Carl, I can't do this. I can't pretend. I can't eat. I've never not been able to eat. I eat when I have the stomach flu!"

"What do you suggest? I work here!" His expression was pained but clearly his mind was made up, at least for now.

"How about seeing if you can stay at David's for awhile? He has plenty of space," I said. David was a newish, wealthy single friend we had met through the Powells. David had built a mansion near the beach. His marriage had ended, although his new girlfriend looked like the twin of the soon-to-be ex-wife. I didn't know how he could tell them apart or why he had made the change.

"You can still come up to work. I just can't do these phony dinners. And sleeping in the same bed is pretty weird."

He didn't say anything. He looked like he was going to cry.

Carl hadn't needed to commute to work for about twelve years, but I certainly wasn't going to move anywhere due to his latest midlife crisis.

I came home from exercise class a few days later. His half of our closet was empty. I felt like I was going to die. I couldn't breathe. I couldn't stand up. I sank to the floor of the closet, curled into a ball and started sobbing. And sobbing. When I finally had no energy left to cry, I slowly picked myself up and took a shower, trying to wash away the horrors of the situation and the puffiness around my eyes. I didn't know what to do.

The phone rang. It was Tom. "Are you okay?"

"No. Carl is gone."

"Gone where?"

"He's met a woman. We're separating. I guess that's what it's called."

"I thought something was wrong. I could feel the vibes weren't right."

He had often tuned in from his perch up the hill to know when I had a cold and needed chicken soup or if one of the boys was having a problem.

"Come on up. I'll give you a glass of wine and we can talk."

I put myself together as best as I could and walked up the driveway. We sat in his little dining room and he poured some white wine into a tall wooden goblet. I was thinking I would rather have a clear glass and realized how silly that I could even bother about that when my whole life was falling apart. I told him the story about what I knew, up until then.

"Well, you'll be fine," he said. He was fond of saying, "Don't worry, nothing will be alright," so I knew when he wasn't joking and that he was concerned. I felt relieved to tell someone what was happening and knew it would help me tell Erik and Swen.

I went home to fix dinner. I hadn't told the boys anything yet. They had grown somewhat accustomed to Carl not being home for dinner in recent weeks, so I waited a bit longer to get up my nerve…and I suppose I also hoped Carl would change his mind. He didn't.

I remember telling Erik in the screen porch. Erik remembers Carl telling him in the living room and that he cried. Swen doesn't remember who told him or where he was.

It was a messy time.

Tom called again a few days later and asked how I was and if I needed anything.

"Well, I just spent $10,000 on my female parts. The hysterectomy cured the pain, and it seems kind of ironic to have it be unused."

He coughed. "Oh. Oh, my."

I knew he cared about me. For about fourteen years I had been very careful not to place myself in a situation that would make Carl feel jealous of Tom, because he knew Tom was fond of me. But now Carl was on his own vision quest. This could be mine.

"Are you there?" I asked.

"Yeah. I can't breathe. I have imagined something like this for years, but never thought it would happen."

"Well?" I prodded.

"Do you want to go up to Neptune's Net for dinner? We can talk about it. I don't want Carl to shoot me...."

"He has no right to shoot you."

"That doesn't mean he won't."

"He doesn't even have a gun!"

"Okay, we can talk about it. What time?"

We drove up the coast and sat outside at the restaurant, even though the autumn air was starting to chill. He brought plates of steamed clams, shrimp and scallops to our outdoor table. He ate most of the meal, since I was queasy from the emotional upset. We didn't talk much.

After dinner, we walked across the highway to the beach. The tide was too high to walk on the sand, so we sat on some rocks and watched the waves roll in.

"So, you really want to do this? You know I've been lusting after you for years, watching you walk to the mail box with your buns hanging out of your short shorts."

"Really? My buns were hanging out?"

"Well, not very far, but enough for the imagination to get cranking. But I also know how close you and Carl have been to each other and…" His voice trailed off. "What if he changes his mind and wants to get back together?"

I thought about this. Somehow, it felt like this was it. Mostly because I wasn't going to put up with Carl's impulsiveness anymore. Some inner strength was brewing, even if I was trying to assuage my grief by running to my neighbor's.

We drove back to Tom's house and made the leap.

We kept leaping about, on and off, for almost fifteen years.

The holidays approached. Carl and I discussed not telling anyone except for Erik and Swen, and sharing the usual celebrations with our parents. Then we decided neither of us was a good enough actor to pull it off.

Patsy and Frank came up, and I asked them to sit with me while I called my parents to tell them about the separation. It was so awkward because my mom had kept up her dislike of Carl all these years. I didn't know if she would jump for joy or have some empathy for me. It was neither.

"Well, it's about time you figured out to separate."

"I didn't figure it out, Mom. It was his decision."

"Oh." That was beyond her ken, and I think it allowed her to have more concern for me.

"If you don't mind, I'd like to skip Thanksgiving dinner together. I'm feeling too upset."

"Okay. I understand," she said, surprisingly. My dad was his usual quiet self. I think he really liked Carl but always restrained himself because of my mom's antipathy toward him.

As it turned out, Thanksgiving was rather festive. I created one of those flotsam and jetsam gatherings of leftover people. I sat next to Tom, and we played footsie. His ex-wife Jennifer was there with her two younger children, Katrina and Jonathan, from a later marriage. Tasha, Erik and Swen were quite delighted with the less formal aspect than dinner with the grandparents. Tom's girlfriend Debby was there, although I didn't know at the time she was a "special" girlfriend, since there had always been ladies coming and going up there. Another friend Jo was there with her new boyfriend who was still married to his wife and mother of five children. There was a lot of laughter and amazement at the collection of souls. I thought, maybe life will go on and in new ways.

Christmas was less successful. Erik, Swen and I spent the morning with my parents and returned home. Carl showed up, drunkish and smoking cigarettes, perhaps enacting some new archetype? He brought some gifts, and we had some for him, but it was probably the worst Christmas ever. I don't recall that he stayed for dinner.

Gina & The Hermes Project
1985 - 1987

I told my girlfriends, Diane and Barbara, about the separation, as we walked out of dance class. They listened and invited me to lunch. I told them I couldn't eat. "We're taking you anyway," Barbara said.

We went to Geoffrey's, the highest-end restaurant in Malibu. It was a warm, clear day and we sat on the deck overlooking the ocean.

"Order whatever sounds appealing," Barbara invited.

Suddenly my appetite returned as I sipped a clear glass of Chardonnay and ate grilled salmon and veggies. It felt like being wrapped in silk, or swimming in warm water, just to be hungry and have something taste good.

"Oh, you guys. Thank you so much for this! I was getting scared. I weigh what I did in junior high school! And it's only been a week!"

I didn't know if I would only have an appetite being in a good restaurant with good girlfriends, but at least it was a start.

As we were nearing the end of our lunch, Barbara, who had created the community center where my class was held, said, "We have a new nonprofit tenant and the director is looking for an administrative assistant. It's called the Hermes Project. Are you interested?"

I had no idea what an administrative assistant did, but I had already attended the Hermes Project's first event in Santa Monica, which was Joseph Campbell giving a Friday night talk, and I knew I was interested, whether I could do the job or not.

"Let's go," Barbara said. The three of us piled into Diane's car, and we drove straight to the center, after chocolate cake and hot coffee.

We knocked on the door of the new office space, a former classroom.

"Come in." welcomed Gina Thompson.

Gina would become a life-changing figure in my new world.

She was tall and slender with blondish hair that was pulled back into a low ponytail, the kind of hair that never slipped out of the rubber band. She was…patrician, a straight aquiline nose and blue eyes, all lined up just right. She was wearing slacks and a cashmere sweater, elegance oozing from her. I was so intrigued that this organization had landed right in the building where I taught my dance class three mornings a week. The upcoming speakers had already been announced, and I knew about every one of them from reading *New Age* magazine. I was a charter member.

"May I have an application for the job?" I asked, after telling her I had already been to the Joseph Campbell evening and that I worked at the other end of the same building.

She pulled one out of a file and handed it to me. "Bring it back on Wednesday morning after your class, and we can talk about what's required."

After dinner that night, I filled out the application, but struggled with a resume. My life had had nothing to do with administrating—assistant or otherwise. Although I did know how to type and I still had my portable Smith Corona 2200, I fretted about it the whole next day.

To be sure, there are others more qualified than I am.

That would be an understatement—just like all of those self-defeating sentences that wandered in and out of my psyche.

I finally made up my mind to take a puffy-covered scrapbook one of my students had made with a Blue Sky dancing icon on the cover. I had filled it with flyers and photos of the dance class, the Blue Sky Women's Retreat days and a picture of me typing the Blue Sky Journal. It was hardly professional, but it showed who I was—or was becoming.

After class, I walked down to Gina's office. The door was open and I walked in, carrying the puffy scrapbook and wearing my leotard tights and the Greek string sandals Carl had made for me. Gina looked as elegant has she had two days earlier. Today, her good hair was loose in a perfect pageboy. She indicated we should sit on the sofa that had been placed in the large room to create a separate area from the desks. I handed her the application first. And then took the risk of passing over the fat scrapbook.

"Pictures are worth thousands of words," I said, placing my hands up and out in a what-else-can-I-say pose.

I watched her closely.
She asked questions.
She laughed.
I knew it was a go.
And it was.

I worked with her for almost three years and later massaged her for another ten.

She had not graduated from college because she married young, and she couldn't type. But she could charm the socks off anyone she spoke to, or solicit money for organizations.

Gina had already been the director for The Center for Healing Arts in Santa Monica, the first place to explore alternative methods of healing for serious illnesses, particularly cancer. Dr. Hal Stone started both organizations.

I learned that Gina had had breast cancer in her early thirties and had been treated with multiple surgeries and severe radiation, which affected her health for the rest of her days.

We connected immediately in the realm of healing and taking charge of our own bodies.

Once Gina and I became better acquainted, I learned her marriage was in a rocky spot, so maybe our liaison occurred to help each other through such a time—although her marriage continued, while mine ended.

It turned out to be one of the richest experiences of my life.

In addition to Joseph Campbell—we hosted him before Bill Moyers did—we had Robert Bly, Jean Shinoda Bolen, Linda Leonard, Dan Millman, Pir Vilayat Khan and many more illustrious thinkers, writers, poets and spiritual teachers. Many of them I had read about in *New Age* magazine. To be with them in person...I was in heaven.

We hosted Friday night talks and daylong Saturday workshops. I was often asked to pick the speakers up at the airport or take them back. Not a problem—this allowed for more one-on-one conversations.

The organization was founded by Dr. Hal Stone, and his mission was to set up and connect healing centers around the world to promote world peace. It was named for Hermes, who was the messenger between the Gods in Greek mythology. I didn't know much about him, but I had been wearing Hermes-like string sandals for most of my adult life, so I felt a great simpatico.

The mission didn't exactly work out as planned. Lack of funds from expected donors prodded Gina to continue inviting these great souls in order to earn enough to keep the office open. I was happy with that solution.

Because of my low wages, I was invited to attend the above-mentioned talks and workshops for free, and also a writing class with Nancy Bacall, a Vipassana meditation class with Shinzen Young and voice dialogue classes with Dr. Hal Stone and his wife, Sidra.

Once we received a call from Esalen Institute in Big Sur informing us they were hosting a group of psychotherapists from Lithuania and inquiring if we would be interested in hosting them in Southern California. Gina was not feeling well at the time and about to say no when I chirped, "Can I host them at my house?" She was a bit skeptical but said okay. I already had created a successful workshop structure as a result of the Blue Sky Women's Retreat Day—morning talks, lunch of homemade bread, huge salad and coffee and cookies in the afternoon. I was becoming the "hostess with the mostess."

I invited my friends who were psychotherapists or counselors to welcome the foreign guests. In the afternoon, Liza Hughes, who was studying with Dr. Stone, invited one person to come to the center of the circle of guests in my living room and tell a dream. While the woman was speaking Lithuanian, her facial expression was telling her story on its own. Liza seemed to get the gist of what the woman was saying and would respond politely in English, and the woman would continue. By now the guest was crying. I probably was, too. I felt as if I were in a Bergmann movie. It was powerful.

The same Lithuanian therapist called me directly a year or two later and asked if she could bring another group to my home. Of course! We had a similarly rewarding day.

One day, I had typed up a flyer to invite guests to join Dr. Stone for a weekend workshop on voice dialogue. We thought we had edited it—both of us reading it. After I had printed 500 copies on green paper, I let out a loud, "Oh, no!"

"What?" Gina demanded.

I had meant to type "Dr. Hal Stone, a Jungian analyst." I reached the end of the line and saw a hyphen in the word 'analyst' and tossed the carriage back to avoid such a grammatical infraction. But, I forgot to go back and delete the first half of 'analyst,' so the flyer read: "Dr. Hal Stone, a Jungian Anal Analyst!"

Gina was appalled, and she worried immediately about the cost of the five hundred pieces of paper. But then it hit her funny bone and the two of us rolled on the floor with uncontrollable laughter, the best healing we could have had.

I then sat and patiently whited-out five hundred 'anal's.

The workshop was a success, and life went on.

In the third year of my time at Hermes, I realized I needed to earn more income. I had always wanted to be a massage therapist. Gina and I discussed my hours and how I could manage both. And, I did.

I trained Ginny to take my place and she actually brought in her computer. I looked at it like it was a foreign object...which it was.

"Here," she said. "I'll pull something up for you to see."

I wanted to look under the desk to see where she was pulling it up from. I restrained myself.

Gina became one of my regular massage clients until she moved to Northern California. We exchanged long, handwritten letters for years. Once I moved to Oregon, I did visit with at her home and spent the night with her. We talked non-stop. Her husband fed us dinner and breakfast. I am so grateful for that time with her, because she became ill and died a year or two later.

Living Next Door
1985

Carl and I had agreed when the shit hit the fan that we would spend a year seeing what happened and not discuss divorce before that time, if it did lead to that. It seemed reasonable. From time to time, we were able to borrow food items we each needed, since it was a long way to the store. Erik and Swen went back and forth as they needed. I moved into their old room, since they were living in little apartments Carl had constructed at the end of the studio. Each had a loft to sleep in and a desk and chair below. We called them condolets. I felt sad to be alone in our big bed and created a new space for myself.

One morning, I was walking home from Tom's when the day was barely dawning, thinking I would be alone. I rounded the bend in the driveway and there was Carl. I don't know why he was there, unless fate had arranged it.

So much for my secret forays to the neighbor's.

It was very awkward.

"Good morning," one of us said first, repeated by the other. I think that was it until he called me a couple of hours later.

"Come over, we need to talk," he said. "I think it's time to get divorced."

He was angry and pacing around his studio. His helper was at the other end, sweeping up clay.

"I thought we were going to wait a year..." I parried.

"Well, I didn't think you were going to take up with Tom so soon! Why are you doing that? We were friends!"

"He's here!" I retorted. "He loves us, all of us. I don't want some stranger hanging around our kids. You've already taken up with someone, whoever that is."

I still didn't know.

"Am I supposed to go to Pacoima to have an affair so your neighborhood is safe?"

I didn't know where Pacoima came from in my mind. It was a poor suburb on the north edge of L.A. County. I'd never been there but it seemed symbolically far away, like Timbuktu or the Amazon rainforest.

Carl paced some more.

Was he seeing the monster he had created with his vision quest?

I went on. "The boys know Tom. They know where I am. They can call me if they need me." At some point, I left.

It felt horrible.

"I'm going to live in the gallery room," he retorted.

Carl had moved back to The Knob from David's. The commute of fifteen minutes was too much for him. He had created a display room in one corner of the long studio for potential customers to view his new, large raku pots, a separate room so the clay dust didn't land on the pots. He moved the pots out and created a bedroom and built a bathroom behind the new room.

My phone rang. It was Carl. "Can you come over?"

"Sure," I said.

What now?

We had gotten over the anger and were living a somewhat normal daily life, able to be available for the boys.

He invited me into his new "home." He had asked for the big bed, since I was no longer sleeping in it. His place was made up, and there were exotic folk paintings on the walls and a few plants. It was livable and somewhat cozy.

"Looks good," I said.

Where had the paintings come from?

"Should we have some champagne?" I suggested.

"I'm not exactly ready to celebrate," he said. "Come over here. Lie down on the bed and look out the window."

This was not a romantic invitation.

He was tentative and looked a bit chagrined.

I did as he suggested. The sliding glass door exactly faced Tom's house.

"Oh," I said.

"I got everything fixed up just right and wanted to take a nap. I lay down and there was my view! How's that for irony?"

"Yeah, pretty ironic," I said. "But at least you still have your sense of humor." We made eye contact, which hadn't been easy.

It was the first time since everything had happened that I felt he was seeing the bigger picture and was willing to look at his part in it. I was touched and relieved and glad he had shared this "awakening" with me.

I continued paying the bills and doing the bookkeeping for our home and his growing business at the Design Center. Some months later, he said he thought he should be doing that now, and I handed him the big, three-on-a-page checkbook and hoped for the best. For years, when I felt anxious about our cash flow and he would assure me it would all be fine, I would say, "But it's me that carries the checkbook!" meaning that literally and figuratively. I carried the worry, since I had to write the checks and balance the checkbook.

Time passed with this new arrangement. I was walking toward the parking area one day when I heard him say, "Hey!"

He was out in the kiln yard, hoisting the giant kiln he had built onto one of his big pots.

"What's up?" I asked.

He cleared his throat. "I wanted to tell you that I understand your anxiety about carrying the checkbook. Now that I'm carrying it, I can't sleep."

"Oh."

I hadn't thought it would be so clear-cut.

"Thank you for telling me. I don't feel like such a wuss with all the grumbling I did over the years."

"I'm sorry I didn't understand. Or didn't listen."

"Well, it's live and learn for both of us. I just love paying my bills on time, and I'm sleeping very well," I grinned. Even with my meager salary at Hermes, I took care of my expenses. He was paying the mortgage as part of our settlement plan, rather than alimony. I chose this plan so that I wouldn't have to ask him for a monthly check.

Helpers

1985 and on...

I was not the only person who was shocked by our separation. It seemed everyone was, and many came to my rescue and opened new doors.

Jennifer, Tom's ex-wife, called me. She was a difficult person, and we had gone through a five-year period of not speaking unless necessary regarding Tasha. But things had softened. Her younger children with a second husband kept her busy, and she was less inclined to be a busybody.

"I know someone who can help you heal," she said. She drove me to a little cottage in the Venice canals where her friend, Franci, was giving psychic readings. I had never had one, but I was game for almost anything at this point.

All I remember from the first visit was that I cried the whole time I sat with her. She was very kind and had a soothing manner. She assured me things would improve. I went to Venice one more time, and then I offered my house for her to give readings so I could trade for mine. She came three or four times a year and helped "clear my aura" of the grief and anger. We always had a festive potluck dinner with whomever wanted to stay for the evening.

I recall one image. After the fence between our two buildings had been erected, Fanci suggested I start visualizing flowers and vines growing on it, covering the bare wood. "See that picture as your new life, emerging and growing."

The next time she visited, I met her in the parking lot.

"I have something to show you." I took her hand and led her to the front yard.

"Look at the fence!" Indeed, there were flowers at its base and a jasmine vine gradually grabbed hold of the wooden slats.

"You see?" she said.

"I do see," I responded. I've been visualizing ever since.

Women's Council

Ruthann had a dream that we were to find elders to guide us. She spent some months asking around to see if anyone knew elders who could teach us. She read books. Then she had another dream. The elders were us!

We both invited all the ladies we knew and met for the first time in Kate's spacious upstairs bedroom in Monte Nido. The windows around two walls opened to oak trees and blue sky. We sat in a circle and Ruthann introduced the talking stick, which we had used at Heartlight School. Only the person holding the stick could speak. Everyone else had to listen. She invited Sue Robin to co-lead the group that would form, bringing her therapeutic expertise to the circle.

Most of us were one side or the other of forty, clearly at crossroads. Four or five of us were newly separated. There were career changes for some, and most were moving into new explorations of life. After two or three meetings, a core group formed. We met monthly for eight years. The support was phenomenal. We took trips to Lake Arrowhead and Sandpoint, Idaho. We attended each other's birthdays, children's bar mitzvahs and later, supported each other through illnesses.

Jack Z.

My life was full and I was doing well most of the time. I had watched Jack, the director of the Heartlight School, deal with situations in ways that were unusual yet helpful.

I think I had been avoiding therapy that first year after the separation because I didn't want to hear someone badmouth Carl, even if I was doing it myself with my girlfriends.

I called Jack. "Can we meet and talk about my separation from Carl?"

"Of course," he responded. He had been an observer of our family during the Heartlight years, and I felt he had a better grasp of our dynamics than a total stranger would.

I can only remember one sentence from our hour-long session, but it was life-changing.

"Laura, you have always carried so much light that Carl just kept getting darker and darker. He finally hooked up with someone darker than he is, so he could start manifesting his light."

Chantal was Haitian and fiery. Definitely not light. Definitely not me.

This was something to think about. I could also see this pattern with my parents, although it was reversed. My dad carried the light and it pissed my mom off, more and more as the years passed. She kept trying to get a rise out of him, and couldn't, so she became meaner and noisier. He just drank more wine and was always pleasant. At least I had the youth and ability to make some internal changes that my parents couldn't manage. And, I had more compassion for my parents and the things that drove me nuts about them, particularly my mom. I could see the similarities between us.

Anne

It was a Sunday morning, and Carl and I had just had a terrible fracas on the phone. I have no idea what the content of it was, other than Chantal seemed to be putting pressure on him to separate himself more from me.

My phone rang. I was mad and sad and had been crying, but I pulled myself together.

"Hello?" I managed to croak out.

"Hi Laura, it's Anne. Do you have time to discuss the upcoming fundraiser?"

We were part of a woman's organization that had formed at the community center.

"Sure," I said, hoping this would distract me.

"Are you okay? Your voice sounds funny."

I let it rip. I spewed out the entire conversation I had had with Carl, which included a lot of…and then he said this…and then he told me that… and, and, and… I was crying again by this time. Once I had run out of breath, I waited for her response. She was one of the nicest people I had ever met, and I knew she would offer succor and sympathy.

She was quiet for a bit. Then she said softly, "Laura…"

"Yes?" I gurgled.

"Laura, what I am really hearing here is that you're feeling like a victim."

I was so shocked, I was speechless. At least the crying stopped.

"What?"

Anne explained that wallowing in my grief wasn't going to get me on my two feet again.

"Life happens," she went on. "You can't fall into such despair that you can't be there for your children, that you can't be a good friend..."

That got me. I sat still and didn't say another word.

A victim? That sounded devastating. And so not me.

Finally, I got myself together enough to thank her for listening and for helping me to see my situation in a new light.

I never forgot that morning. It was another step I took to regain my self.

Years later, I heard she opened a bead shop in a nearby town. I went in and told her how she had likely saved my life--or at least my sanity. I thanked her. She thanked me for telling her.

"It's just what I saw. I knew you would pick yourself up."

"A LITTLE BOOK ABOUT THE HUMAN SHADOW" BY ROBERT BLY

Gina gave me a copy of the book after we hosted Robert Bly for a weekend event. The Friday night talk and the weekend workshop were enlightening, but the tiny book spoke to me directly.

Bly talked about how from the time we are born we are told not to do things in a certain manner and to be the way our parents, teachers and even our peers thought we should be. Unless we were particularly strong and clear, we tossed the comments into a bag we carried over our shoulder, and it became heavier and heavier.

When we were about twenty, it was likely we would meet someone who manifested all the things we had thrown into our bags, and they recognized us in the same way: we had been carrying their stuff, as well. In our case, I was the pleasant girl who always pleased her parents and teachers. For Carl, he was the rebel artist who had forgone stability and safety. We were drawn to each other like moths to light. Together, we felt comfortable, met and heard. We fell in love, but with whom? As Bly noted in the book, the two of us together did not even make one whole person.

For twenty years, it worked for us as a family. I revelled in Carl's art and outspokenness. He felt blessed by my stability and ability to "take care of things." According to Bly, when the forties show up, the material in the bags starts to rattle; it wants out. It wants to manifest what is stuffed in the bag.

For me, it started in small ways. I wanted to explore creativity for myself and to be able to speak up for my rights. He wanted to create a business and wealth and have nice clothes and a good car. No more Bohemia for him. I would have to embrace the artistic/healing life for myself.

I was surrounded by people in their early forties who were separated or newly divorced. The couples who were not divorced were either grumbling at each other or becoming quieter. Bly's little book became a bible for me. I didn't feel like such a failure, as if I had done something wrong, that Carl had done something wrong. I spent more time thinking we were waking up and setting each other free—I wasn't able to hold onto this new self every minute of the day, but more often than not.

Mary

I had heard about Reiki, an Asian healing method, in my meanderings in the New Age world. A very sweet and petite English woman named Mary attended some of the events at the Hermes Project. When I found out she was a Reiki Master, I asked her if she would teach a class if I could round up the students. She said yes, and we held it at my home. First Level I and later Level II. The teachings provided ways to heal one another and to effect self-healing, and I used it all the time, especially if I fell off track or became angry or afraid.

Later, after I attended massage school, Mary and I began trading sessions of Reiki. She was not only a master of touch and teaching, but she was also very intuitive. She often popped out words of wisdom while she treated me.

One day, I told her about my initial menstruation experience at the age of twelve. It started in December and didn't stop until June, following two hospitalizations. The medical reason was that one in 10,000 women had irregular onset and cessation of menses. I was one in 10,000. I thought that was it; that I knew everything I needed to know.

Mary didn't think so.

"So, your mother didn't want you to become a woman," she said, after I had told my story.

"Yeah, she never wanted me to grow up," I responded.

"No," Mary went on, "She didn't want you to become a woman."

I sat with that, not sure what she meant or what the connection was with the bleeding.

I had already told her about the unusual situation in my childhood household. My mother went to work on the swing shift when I was eight years old, leaving me in the care of my dad from the time he got home from work until bedtime. I always thought this was a good plan because I got along better with my dad than my mom. Mary's hit was that once I began menstruating, I was no longer a child and maybe this situation could become dangerous.

Maybe my psyche thought it was dangerous and it told me to bleed and bleed so my mom would get the message. It sounded kind of far-fetched at the moment, but it explained some of my behaviors that were unconscious to me at the time.

I was my dad's de-facto partner. We shared dinner every evening, going out to eat on Monday and Thursdays. He helped me with homework. And then, on the weekends, my mom was there and I had to share. I wondered if this was a source of my being lenient with Carl and his forays with other women and that I so easily entered into a relationship with Tom when he already had a girlfriend—once again, me during the week, and she on the weekends. It took awhile for this to sink in and take effect, but I continued to ponder Mary's thoughtful insights as the years passed.

Bette

Bette lived in Ruthann's neighborhood and joined the Women's Council. She was writing poetry and a memoir. I told her about a writing class at the Hermes Project, led by Nancy Bacall. I hadn't thought of myself as a writer, after my failed attempt at my bio of Carlos, but I was allowed to attend the Hermes events for free. We signed up together. The class opened new creative doors for me and cemented my friendship with Bette.

After the class ended, we formed a weekly group with two other women,

April and Diana. I began writing personal essays. Bette continued with her memoir. Memories of her childhood abuse had emerged. We started having coffee most days after dance class. All of our inner life was burbling up in our writing exercises and as we parsed our stories over coffee.

Travel Helped, Too!

1985 and on…

BADGER PASS

Shortly after the first Christmas, which was painful beyond description, we were invited by a group of families in Decker Canyon to go to Badger Pass in Yosemite for a very inexpensive ski week. Diane and her boys came, as well as Tasha and about fifteen to twenty other locals. We had never skied before.

Ski classes were included in the package deal, along with lodgings in the valley and the bus ride up to the lifts. We each started on the bunny slope and by day two, Erik, Swen and I had moved on to bigger challenges. It was exhilarating. I was able to get down the slightly steeper slopes by singing "Winter Wonderland" out loud, so I wouldn't think about which foot was supposed to turn in what direction, and when. Somehow, Carl thought family vacations were too much work, and we had only taken a couple over the twenty years. This one was a snap and we laughed and enjoyed ourselves.

DENMARK

Because Erik was sixteen and Swen was now twelve, I figured it wasn't likely that we would be traveling together for long. I announced that I would like to take them to Denmark so they could learn something about their roots. Alice heard me and donated five hundred dollars to the cause. We found cheap charter flights and flew to my dad's homeland.

We visited many households and my sons graciously sat through long dinners with multiple courses and not much English being spoken. We visited Tivoli Gardens and drove through the countryside where locals set bonfires to keep witches and evil at bay on *Sankt Hans Aften* (June 23). We also spent a week with my younger cousin, Peter, and his family at their beach house, where English was spoken.

I felt the trip helped remove certain boundaries that had been in place, unconsciously, for a long time, and for Erik, Swen and me to be a new family in a new way. We had already been skiing at Yosemite. We found it easy to jump into the car and go for hamburgers and a movie, without Carl urging us to hurry up. But getting on a plane and flying almost to the other side of the world, where a different language was spoken, opened doors to new possibilities.

Idaho

By the time the second Christmas approached, Michael and Ruthann had moved to Sun Valley, Idaho, for good. We made plans to visit them. Michael drew a detailed map of how to drive there.

"Go through Las Vegas, but be sure to get gas. Drive about ninety miles to Highway 93 and turn left. Continue north to Alamo, which is the best place to spend the night."

We followed directions, except for the gas part. My Toyota Squareback got such good mileage. I may also have had the notion that if I could drive faster, I'd get to Alamo quicker and get gas there. I am sure I did not get this notion from my father who told me the minute I turned sixteen that he would rescue me from any automotive mishap except running out of gas, as that would be a self-inflicted wound. And no one had mentioned to me that driving faster uses more gas.

We ran out of gas about fifty miles south of Alamo. I didn't know the coughing sounds and lurching of the car were symptoms, except that it stopped. The gas gauge read empty.

Erik hitchhiked and caught a ride right away with a carload of men dressed in camouflage jackets. We were in duck hunting country. Swen and I played hangman and tic-tac-toe while we waited and walked across the road where we could see a small lake surrounded by weeds and rushes. The same people were kind enough to bring Erik back with the can of gas.

After pouring the gas, Erik said, "You are not going to believe Alamo."

"What do you mean?"

"Just wait and see."

I don't know what I was picturing—not an Army fort like the historical one in Texas, but since Michael was so clear we should stop there, I did imagine it was a town. It was not. It was a motel and two gas stations, one with a trucker's cafe. Somehow the tension of my gas-error, the safety of Erik returning from his foray in the middle of the Nevada desert with camo-dressed hunters, and the size of the non-town, set us into hysterics. We laughed and laughed, the sputtering kind that when we tried to stop we were making spitting noises and grasping our bellies.

Traveling safely to Sun Valley on our own and back, navigating the gas situation—mild as it was—opened more doors to our self-sufficiency as a new family constellation. We skied—me not very successfully on the very steep slopes—and saw new territory. We made several more trips to visit the Saphiers—without running out of gas.

Over the Fence

1986

I finally found out who the "other woman" was.

During a chat with Carl, I said, "It's Chantal, isn't it?"

"Yeah. How did you figure it out?"

"The island art. Studying French. Remembering when she took us to Beau Rivage on Bastille Day and snuck out and paid the bill. The Haitian jackets she gave to me and to your mom? Kinda overly familiar for being new acquaintances. I don't know why it took me so long."

We had met her and her alleged husband, Peter, when they came up to buy pots, which Peter had seen in a gallery in town. He wanted them for Chantal's clothing stores, which were on the Westside, elegant and expensive.

We plied them with wine and cheese, to encourage the pottery sales, not to induce an affair!

They invited us to their home for dinner. They told us that they were divorced because they slept at different times of the day and he had some shady financial deals that worried Chantal. But they functioned as a couple. They were both charming and colorful in dress and attitude. She was from a wealthy family in Haiti, he from Jamaica.

"Why were you so hesitant to tell me?" I asked.

"Because Peter flew into a rage when he found out Chantal and I had gotten together and I didn't know what was going to happen. He ruined her business. I didn't know if he'd come up here and cause trouble."

"Yikes!" Peter had gifted me with a bottle of Opium perfume, the only fragrance I ever liked. It was part of his nefarious dealings, but I didn't know that then. He was gentlemanly during my few visits with him.

"Is he still raging?" I asked.

"No, he's calmed down. Chantal moved to Santa Monica. That's where I've been going on the weekends."

Carl knocked on the door one day and said, "I want to build a fence between our buildings."

"Okay," I said. "Why now and what for?"

"I'd like Chantal to move up here. The drive into Santa Monica every weekend is taking a toll on me."

Poor thing. Maybe you shouldn't be having an affair with a woman in town. But I kept my mouth shut.

Instead I said, "Well that should be interesting. She knows I don't plan to go anywhere, doesn't she?"

"Yeah. She's not thrilled about that, but willing to give it a try."

"Well, show me how you see the fence. Will there be a gate?"

"Of course."

The fence was built, and he walled-off more space in the studio for additional rooms.

The next phase was beginning.

From parking lot to garden

Once the fence was up, I realized I had boundaries to create a garden outside the front door. I borrowed Tom's truck to drive along the canyon roads and load up chunks of shale that had fallen from the cliffs. I used the rocks to create borders and started planting. Erik built a little arbor coming off the fence to walk under. I planted some grape vines, with visions of dangling grapes.

Our writer friend Victor arrived one day. He was enraged.

"How did you let Carl do this?" he shouted. Victor was a shouter.

"Do what?" I asked.

"Look how far you have to walk to your car?" He gesticulated toward the lower lot and the distance to my house.

"But Victor, look what's happening here! I'm making it pretty. This whole area used to be full of cars. Doesn't this look better?"

"You've got a point, I guess. But what about lugging your groceries up here?"

"I got a shopping cart, and I pull it up the ramp that we made."

"Oh."

"Plus, Victor, I got the view. Look! And see, here's a gate, the boys can walk back and forth."

Victor and Barbara separated soon after we did, and also continued living next door to each other.

Another visitor knocked at my front door one evening. I had never seen the man before.

"Carl asked if we could borrow some eggs. We're cooking an omelet and are short."

"Sure, come on in," I motioned him into the living room.

"Wow!" he exclaimed. "You got the wheel and he got the shaft!"

He was looking at my view, noting that Carl could only see the backside of the fence.

"Yeah, well, it wasn't exactly my idea, but I do love my view. Expansive, isn't it?" I grinned.

There were parts of this new life that were kind of fun. I gave him the eggs and went about my tasks.

One day I was walking down the driveway and Carl and Chantal were standing outside the kiln yard, which was now also fenced in. This was good. It had looked very industrial and now between the fence and the pepper tree I could only see the top of the giant raku kiln.

One of them looked up and saw me and they ducked into the kiln yard like they were afraid of me. This was the first time I had seen Chantal since she had moved up to The Knob. It didn't feel good to see them running away, and I decided to put a stop to that.

I stormed through the gate. Well, maybe I opened the gate and walked through it. They looked terrified, especially Carl. I don't know if he thought I would yell some more or throw pots, but he clearly didn't have the thought that peacemaking was on my mind.

Chantal made an effort to smile. I walked over to her and put my arms around her. She relaxed.

"Look!" I started. "If we're gonna try this experiment, please don't make me feel like I'm an enemy in my own yard! We can be civil and friendly, can't we?"

Chantal started laughing, clearly relieved. Carl was still standing back, blinking rapidly and not saying a word. I looked at him. "You too! I'm not going to bite anyone!"

This began thirteen more years of being next-door neighbors. Chantal gave me clothes when she found something she thought I would like. Some years later when I had a "city boyfriend" with a business, she really decked me out so I didn't look like a hippie exercise teacher.

I taught her to use a Macintosh computer. Her English was not great despite having been in the U.S. for over a decade. I think she took advantage of it because it sounded cute. "What? How you say?" kind of thing. But she was smart and picked up the Mac more easily than I had. The Mexican workers were very wary when they saw us together, I think because such an arrangement would not happen in their culture. But they got used to us being friendly.

We had occasional dinners together. We all went on about our lives on Barney's Knob, on both sides of the fence.

Divorcing
1986 – 1989

LADY LAWYERS

Sometime later we decided to proceed with a divorce, but were unsure how we would do it. Carl knocked on the front door and handed me an envelope.

"Here, read this," he said. "A friend of Chantal's wrote it up."

I opened the envelope and tried to read the contents. It was so full of words like *whereas, aforesaid, waiver* and *forthwith*, that I got an instant headache.

"Carl, this is not going to work for us. Our situation is different. We're normal people. We barely own anything that would require such obfuscation." I was ready to cry. I couldn't believe our twenty-year marriage was being reduced to this.

"Obfuscation?"

"See, it's communicable, these silly large words just separate us instead of letting us achieve something workable."

He walked back through the gate in the fence, shrugging his shoulders.

After trashing the first legal document, I decided to visit a lawyer and see if there was a more humane way we could approach this. I was determined to not end up like Carl's parents who never spoke to each other again, even at their daughter's funeral.

There was a female lawyer in Malibu who had helped a friend when she got divorced. I explained our complicated situation, that we both needed stay on our property, about the other woman and how to deal with our meager finances that were growing a bit.

"It's simple," she said. "You sell the property, divide the money in half, and it's done."

"But, we don't want to do that. We both love how special The Knob is, and we have already figured out how to live next door to each other. Carl can't leave because he can't set up his giant kilns any old place. And I'm not going anywhere."

She waved her arm at me like brushing away a fly. "Don't be silly," she said in exasperation. "Sell the place and you're done."

And this was her advice? I chose her because she wasn't some dude in a three-piece suit with shiny shoes. Shouldn't she have my wants, needs, desires and my best interests in helping me?

I sat there, stunned for a moment. I was in the wrong place, got up, left and never saw her again.

Another woman lawyer was recommended to me by a friend, who had a friend, who had worked with her. Her specialty was women's issues, and I made an appointment. I was very optimistic. Surely, she would understand.

She was very sweet, well coiffed and had a nice office on the Valley side of The Knob. I explained my situation to her, expecting nods of agreement. They did not appear. She was definitely more gracious than the first lawyer, but basically said the same thing: sell it and be done. She also indicated that if Carl wouldn't agree to sell, we would take him to court.

"It is your right as a woman, after all," she said, smiling.

It didn't feel right for any human being and would certainly not allow a family to have conversations with each other for the rest of their lives.

I thanked her for her time and left.

DIY Divorce

Someone told me a about a DIY divorce book. I bought the book: *How to Do Your Own Divorce*, by NOLO Press. It was way cheaper than the first visits with either lawyer. I notified Carl I was on it and it would be taken care of soon. Or, so I thought.

I filled out the documents as directed. I still had all of our personal paperwork and it seemed easy. I mailed the packet to the court and went on about my daily life. My massage practice was growing. The boys seemed to be doing well at school. Swen attended Malibu Park Junior High and Erik was at Agoura High. Tom and I were having fun, in between my bouts of anxiety and wondering how all this came about.

Months passed and I received a packet from the court. It said I needed to include the such-and-such, or the this-and-that. I complied and mailed it in again.

Pottery Shards

One day I was sitting in my dining room painting my toenails. Carl knocked and asked if he could come in.

"Sure. If you don't mind the smell of nail polish remover, have a seat."

He said, "I think I'll stand."

Uh-oh.

"Now what?" I said out loud.

"Well, Chantal really likes you and all, but her family thinks this is a very weird situation." He was pacing back and forth now—on the plywood floor that he had painstakingly burned intricate designs into with a torch, after we removed the outdoor carpet.

"Her family? They live in Haiti? What do they care?"

"Well, I spoke to my dad," he went on. "He said he would loan me $15,000 to give you so you could move down to Point Dume where all your friends are."

I didn't speak, but my blood started to boil in a way it never had. I knew I had low blood pressure, but it occurred to me I might have a stroke anyway.

"What do you think?" he said, innocently, though I could tell he was nervous. He was pacing faster and turning quickly. I noticed he was wearing shiny loafers instead of clay-studded boots.

I jumped up, not caring if I knocked my polish jars over and started yelling. *Yelling!*

I had never felt so angry, nor have I felt since.

"Fuck you!" I shouted. "Who do you think you are, offering me a pittance for my half of the place? I don't want to live on the Point! My friends come up here and love it! I love it here.! This is my home! You leave if you don't like it!"

By now he was backing toward the front door, trying to shush me.

"The workers are going to hear you. Stop it!"

"I don't care about your workers. Fuck them, too!"

I followed him, yelling, until he ducked into the studio.

I didn't know what to do with rage, but I was sure having it. I walked out the kitchen doors onto the top step leading down to the patio. I was overcome with a need to throw things. The area was dotted with large pots—we kept the ones with cracks or blown-out bottoms, so I knew I wouldn't be losing much of value.

I stomped down the stairs and picked up the first piece of pottery I could get my hands on and stomped back up. I threw it as forcefully as I could onto the cement. It made delicious crashing sounds, which I could barely hear because I was still yelling. Screaming. Swearing.

Down again, and up again, throwing everything I was able to lift and carry up the stairs. Some of the pots were really big, but it seemed I had that extra strength you read about when moms can lift cars off their children. It was very rewarding and noisy. While I felt lost in the rage, I still had access to some part of my brain that did not pick up the pottery that I liked. I also was able to remember that my writing class was going to take place at four o'clock. I kept my eye on my watch and stopped in time to take a shower—by now I was dripping with sweat and my voice was as hoarse as a frog—and I drove calmly to the Point for my class. I felt renewed and cleansed. There were plenty more pots around should I need them in the future. I didn't.

When I returned home that night, I noticed that the patio had been swept clean. There was not a chunk of broken pottery in sight. It made me chuckle.

A few days later, I was walking toward the parking lot when Carl said over the fence, "Hey. I guess you were not pleased with my offer." He had a sly grin.

I looked up at him and said, "No, I wasn't," and continued on my way.

I felt something heal between us. One of his complaints about me had been that I remained even-tempered all the time, unless I was premenstrual. Maybe it was too late for the marriage, but I knew I was pulling some parts of myself together. Maybe he was, too.

Erik told me later that he had parked below and started walking up the ramp when he heard me yelling. He returned to his car and stayed with friends for a few days. The incident became a Knob legend that we retold over the years.

The Stipulation

The DIY packet returned several more times from the court. One of the difficulties was how to describe splitting the property, which could not be divided because of land-use ordinances. It could not be made smaller than the ten acres, most of which were vertical, on which our buildings sat. I explained this to Carl and made another attempt with the documents. Several years had passed since we separated.

I came out the front door on my way to my monthly Women's Council meeting. Carl was pushing through the gate as if he had been waiting for me.

"Here," he said, handing me a large envelope. He turned and walked back to his side of the fence.

I sat down on the front steps and opened it. The front page was titled: "The Stipulation for the Bifurcation of the Dissolution of the Marriage."

How the hell did twenty years of intimacy, laughter, good sex and raising two sons come to this legalese crap?

But the words were so funny that the rage didn't return. I took the package with me to the council. We shared our monthly stories. Sue had brought materials to decorate T-shirts. I went right to work and wrote the silly words in script around the shirt with paint that was supposed to pouf up with heat. I had the words intertwined with grape vines and leaves. It was a work of art. Alas, when I put it in the microwave to pouf up the paint, it turned brown. I never got to wear it, but it let me dispell the absurdity of the situation.

The next time the DIY documents returned, they were complete, except for one thing: the instructions said the blue soft paper that held the stapled pages together was folded incorrectly!

I happened to be going to a summer party that night. I spotted Bette's husband, who was a local judge, and told him about the latest snafu. First, he took his cocktail napkin and started folding it. Next, he took my cocktail napkin and inserted it into his. "Here's what they mean. For some damn reason, it has to be a half-inch in this direction and the fold has to be…but wait a minute, this is crazy! You've been at this for over three years?"

"Uh, huh," I said.

"You bring me the document on Monday morning, and I'll take care of it."

I did.

He called me in a few days and said, "I gave 'em hell. I told them here we have citizens who are trying to be civil to each other and save the court money…this is ridiculous! I have your completed document here. You are technically divorced!"

I thanked him profusely, but didn't know whether to laugh or cry. I was relieved it was done. But also, *it was done*.

I called Carl. "Meet me at the gate," I said. I handed him the thick envelope. He looked at it and looked at me. We hugged and both of us got choked up. We made a date to have dinner together.

Elissa

1989 to the present

"Mom, I met an intriguing woman. I say woman, because she is thirty!" Erik was nineteen at the time. "Can you meet us at Lucy's El Adobe on Melrose?"

"Of course. What time?" I was eager to meet anyone he was interested in because he hadn't introduced me to any girls yet. Plus, I had massage clients in the Hollywood Hills and would pass nearby.

"Good. Her name is Elissa. You'll like her. And her middle name is Laura."

How could I resist? I agreed to meet them the next day for lunch.

We met at El Adobe. After ordering enchiladas verdes, my favorite Mexican dish, we became acquainted. She was pretty in a European way and had a great sense of humor. Her hair was the same dark brown as Erik's. I learned her mother was from Romania and was an art curator, and her father had been a documentary film director from New York. They had moved to Laurel Canyon in order to curate an exhibit when Elissa and her brother, Ethan, were very young. I felt comfortable with her.

Erik and Elissa began telling me how they met. Erik was working at a sound studio owned by Patsy's niece. He had moved to Hollywood to pursue acting, which had not manifested. The niece spotted him on a street corner and invited him to come and see their studio. She was looking for a maintenance person, but said she would train him as a recording engineer. He was waiting for that to happen when Elissa showed up. She had been hired as the studio manager, but within two weeks she knew the job was not for her. She had managed a large studio in New York City for ten years and had the skills to discern if she was a good fit or not.

In the short time they both worked at the studio, they began chatting and discovered they both loved horses. They met to ride in the nearby hills, followed by lunch at Lucy's.

In one conversation, Erik said, "I would like to have an affair with a married woman. The single girls I have dated take me home to meet their families after a few weeks, and I'm not interested in marriage. I'm only 19!"

Elissa responded, "Well, I am married!" She was at the end of a ten-year marriage, but not yet divorced.

Then Erik shared, "I went to Elissa's apartment so she could show me a picture of a guy she was telling me about in her yearbook. When she found the page with his photo. I saw that standing next to the guy was Jack Zimmerman!"

That was a surprise! He was the director of Heartlight School that Erik and Swen attended and had become an important person in our family. Elissa reported that Jack was the director of her high school. I felt we were more connected than just sharing the name Laura.

"Furthermore," she went on, "I had a psychic reading shortly after I arrived in Los Angeles. She said she saw a building with thick glass windows. I would go there but not stay. The sound studio has such windows. We figure the psychic's vision was about me meeting Erik."

It looked like a done deal to me.

The Ranch

About a year later, Elissa received a call from a longtime friend who had been living in Idaho. She wanted to leave her ranch for awhile to pursue her career. "Do you know anyone who would like to be a caretaker there?"

"Let me get back to you," Elissa replied.

She called Erik. "How'd you like to caretake a ranch in Idaho for a year?"

"Sounds good to me. When?"

Erik drove up there in April. Elissa followed after she had given notice at her job. I followed them both in August, stopping in Sun Valley to pick up Ruthann. As we drove on the long road to the ranch, we saw Elissa riding toward us on a horse. She was wearing a rose-colored V-neck shirt and jeans and looked totally at home. We celebrated Erik's twenty-first birthday.

They were responsible for tending a dozen horses, three goats and a flock of egg-laying chickens, as well as keeping intruders off of the ranch. Herds of elk wandered through the back yard, and mountain lions, badgers and marmots appeared. The land was bordered by a rushing creek on one side, the Salmon River on another and forest around the rest of the perimeter. There were hiking trails in every direction and a natural hot spring that flowed into a hot pool, which flowed into a very large swimming pool.

Erik and Elissa stayed for seventeen years instead of one. I drove there every Christmas and summer for two weeks each time. It was an extra-added benefit that my dear pal Ruthann was on the way to and from the ranch.

IAN

Around year six, Elissa started feeling that her biological clock was ticking faster and faster. Pregnancy ensued. The due date was May eighteen.

Around May first, Elissa called to say, "The doctor told me I'm effacing and that birth is imminent. Can you come up now?" We had already decided I would come for the birth and her mom would come to care for Elissa and the baby.

I told my dance class and massage clients I would be gone for a few days and got on a plane instead of into my car. I had never been to Idaho in the spring and loved seeing all the fields of daffodils on the way from the airport.

Elissa and I settled into a routine at her boss's condo in Sun Valley, so we would be close to the hospital. We waited and waited. We ate at most of the restaurants in town, since we didn't want to stock up on groceries. We read JoAnn Mapson cowboy novels. I responded belatedly to Christmas letters and was quite pleased with all the free time. Elissa not so much. She was growing bigger and more uncomfortable each day.

"Surely, he will be born by *Cinco de Mayo*...or Grandpa Erik's birthday on the seventh. Or Carl's birthday on the thirteenth. Or Mother's Day, for sure!"

Finally, three weeks after my arrival, Elissa began having contractions.

We called Erik, and as soon as he arrived we went to the hospital. More waiting ensued, but on May eighteenth, his original due date, Ian Janco

Gillberg was born. Erik brought him out of the delivery room so I could hold him for a minute. He was beautiful. We both wept looking at him.

Divorced

1989

I decided I would create a photo album for Carl that we could look at together at our "divorce dinner"—sort of like a life-review but with no one having to die anytime soon. Instead: the death of the marriage. I had been the keeper of our family photographs. Our scrapbooks were all the kind that had plastic see-through sheets covering the pictures. Nothing was glued down.

I put all the old books out on the dining room table the following weekend. The house was full of Swen's friends and the atmosphere was cheerful. I was glad because I didn't know if going down memory lane would pull me apart or lift me up.

I found that I often stopped to show someone a photo…Swen at Lion Country Safari or Carl sitting in an outhouse at Charmlee Park with the door open.

Several of the young people asked, "What are you doing?"

"I'm creating a photo album of our life here to give to Carl at our divorce dinner."

"Oh."

No one seemed to get the concept, but I felt healed by the experience, kind of like walking through twenty years in twenty minutes once it was done. I knew cameras were out when fun events were happening, like birthday parties or Easter egg hunts. But no one snapped a photo of an argument or the roof leaking onto my cousin's paintings. But still…it was a life, and it was a fun life for the most part.

Carl told me to come to his place the night of our divorce dinner. He had set the camera on a tripod to take a picture of us for the occasion. He took several shots using a timer, running to stand next to me before the flash went off. Chantal had given me a new dress to wear, but she was not around to send us off. I was glad for that.

I requested that we not eat in Malibu, where we were likely to run into old friends and have to explain. So, we went down the backside of the mountain to Matter of Taste, a longtime favorite cafe. Good food and art gallery in one place. I placed the photo album on the far side of the table and we ordered our dinner.

We chatted about mundane things for a bit…the boys, what to tell the people we bought our house from, news of the friends we still shared. We split a bottle of wine, and I know he had had some drinks before, so there was a dull edge, covering the anxiety, the purpose of the booze I guess.

When we finished eating, I asked, "Can we look at the pictures now?" It seemed to me the perfect way to summarize and complete our marriage.

Carl was quiet, looking at the album. "No. I can't do that right now. I'll take it home and look at it, I promise. Thank you for making it."

"But why?"

"Just can't. Too much."

I was disappointed. I had felt so much more uplifted by our family photos than I had expected when I was creating the album. I wanted him to feel the same way. But he didn't.

We got in the car and started up the road.

Now that it was dark and we couldn't really see each other, Carl said, "I want to thank you for all the good sex we had."

I was stunned. I thought our sex life was good. We fit together, I had delicious orgasms, but I had no other twenty-year period to compare it with. The sex I had had during the last four years was more like maintaining some sense that I was still valuable or attractive. Except for Tom, it was a series of odd connections, none related to ongoing daily life. I had always thought of making love as the glue, the way we could come together after an argument or when we were scared about our finances or when we had a free night with the boys gone somewhere.

"Well, thank you," was about all I could muster. "Same to you," I added. It made me wonder about his last four years, but of course that seemed way too personal to ask, especially when he couldn't even look at the photos. I didn't ask.

But since we were moving into a sharing moment that didn't quite happen at the dinner, I said, "I want to apologize for not standing up for you better when my mom was so snarky and critical." It was one of my greatest regrets, both that I hadn't stood up for him, but also that I had never spoken about it.

"Your mom didn't bother me so much. It was your dad. I knew how much you loved him, and I felt jealous."

"You felt jealous of my dad?" I was astounded. I didn't know that but remembered a time when we were in a Mexican restaurant and I had been asking the mariachis to play certain songs. Carl mumbled, "That tall skinny guy is like your dad…that's why you're asking him for songs." We were with friends, so it wasn't a moment to ask what he meant. And there was probably tequila involved, so I forgot about the incident. I did love my dad, but he was in a very different category than Carl, and I could not understand his jealousy. I wondered what else we hadn't said to each other, but by now we were nearing our driveway.

We got out of the car and hugged. We hadn't had a real kiss in four years, and I guessed we weren't going to have one now.

"Thank you for honoring this landmark with me," I said. "Don't forget to look at the photo album."

"Thank you for thinking of it. I will."

He told me a few days later that he had looked at the pictures and was glad to have them.

A few weeks passed. I had a sore throat and felt a cold coming on. I called next door to see if I could borrow some chicken soup. Carl said sure, and I went through the gate into the studio. Carl handed me a can of chicken noodle soup, and we were standing there chatting for a moment. Chantal came out and greeted me. And then their secretary came out of her office when she heard Chantal's voice.

"Well, congratulations Mrs. Gillberg," she said smiling. She wasn't looking at me, who I believed was Mrs. Gillberg, despite the divorce. I was confused until I turned toward Chantal whose eyes were bulging out and she had her hand over her mouth.

I got it, mentally and viscerally. They had gotten married. I still have no idea what happened, but I felt like I had been shot or stabbed. Pain ripped through me, worse than any of our previous separations or issues. I turned and ran home and threw myself on the bed in the screen porch. It didn't make sense. We had been separated for four years and had finally celebrated the legal divorce. Why did I feel like dying?

Carl came into the porch and squatted down on the floor next to me. "I'm sorry you heard it like that. Chantal is on her hands and knees crying. We were just out at my dad's in Palm Springs, and my dad suggested we get married and that he could invite their minister over. So we did. That's why we didn't tell anyone. We didn't even get dressed up."

I was crying and aching and thinking I was going nuts. He had his hand on my shoulder. I put my hand on his.

Many Changes

1989

I decided it was time to go to therapy. Several of my friends were seeing a therapist named Robert. I made an appointment with trepidation. Gale was in town and went into Westwood with me for support. I cried and cried at the first session, but continued thereapy for a couple of years. He used holotropic breathing as a technique to rid oneself of hidden demons. The loud, pounding music did make me cry and wail, but it was not as relieving as I expected, and certainly not uplifting.

The therapist was shocked when I told him my mother went to work on the afternoon shift when I was eight, leaving me to my dad for homework time and dinner. I had always thought this was a boon to my daily life. My dad was easygoing. He had no idea of what I wore to school, so I could pile skirts on top of petticoats. My mom was critical and needed things to match.

"But why did she do that?" the therapist asked. "Was it a financial necessity?"

"No. She said it was so there would always be one parent available for me." It made sense to me and I never doubted it.

I discussed this with Erik. He asked my mom about it. She told him she loved the afternoon shift because she was the lead-lady and had power, which she had never had before.

When I brought this discrepancy up with her, it hurt her feelings, and I was sorry that I had mentioned it. I understood my therapist's dismay once I found out that half of my girlfriends had been molested by a family member. It was a perfect set-up for that, but it didn't happen. I remained pleased that my dad had more or less raised me.

The holotropic breathing was supposed to lead to a clean slate. It made sense at first, but after awhile I felt I didn't really want a clean slate. I liked some of my demons, and I quit.

Tom moved to Colorado. He claimed he always planned to move once Tasha was out of high school. She had not only graduated but had married Tommy, her co-worker at the restaurant the year before. She wore a gorgeous white gown and cut into a five-layered cake. I danced until my hair was dripping. Erik and Swen drank until they were blotto.

Never take two teenagers to a wedding with an open bar.

Somehow, Erik drove us home.

Never go to a wedding where your lover's girlfriend is quietly sitting at another table.

Once Tom was gone, he wrote to say that he had invited the girlfriend back to Colorado and then married her. "It was just something I had to do. She was forty-five and had never been married...and I got drunk at the wedding..."

Blah blah blah.

It was as if he didn't want to let me go, but had. I was angry and heartbroken.

Tom was such a puzzle in my life. He had been a loyal and supportive next-door neighbor for eighteen years, and then a regular lover for another four or five years. He was funny and all of us adored him. One day, he came down to our house with a friend driving his truck. He was delivering his old piano to us for Swen to take lessons. Tom was riding in the bed of the truck playing the piano all the way down the driveway.

At times, Tom and Tasha would come down for spaghetti dinners. They always turned into spaghetti sucking contests, seeing who could get the longest noodle sucked up without it breaking. This of course splattered red sauce all over the sucker's face and clothes. We all laughed and laughed.

Tom came to one of our lamb roast parties, even though he was not very social. Someone squealed, "Spider! Big spider!" It was indeed a large tarantula ambling across the lawn toward the fire. Tom calmly walked over to the critter, scooped it up in his giant hand and lightly tossed it off the end of the lawn. Everyone watched, mouths agape. He was always just a little bigger than life, in his physical size and in his ability to have fun and get us to laugh.

I wanted to be mad at him forever because of marrying Debby, but I couldn't. He called about two years after he left. "Can we have dinner?" he asked.

I had just given a couples-massage workshop and didn't feel like cooking.

Lame excuse for my trying to stay angry.

"Sure," I said, positive I would keep my clothes on.

We went out to eat and chit-chatted, and all was well.

He brought me home. My friend April had introduced me to the Gipsy Kings, which were sweeping the nation with their romantic and lively songs.

"Have you heard of the Gipsy Kings?" I asked.

Surprisingly, he had not. I put the album on, and soon we were dancing. And soon we were taking off our clothes.

I later found out that Swen and his friends came home early from a concert and arrived on the porch when I was having a noisy orgasm. They turned around and left—in a hurry.

The next day, he asked, "How was your evening was with Tom?"

"Fine," I replied. "Very platonic."

I had not only embarrassed myself and Swen but flat-out lied to him. The story was retold, and the friends called me "Foghorn" for years.

Tom and I started seeing each other again whenever he came to L.A. for work.

Workshops, Gale, Travels, Heart Openings & Closings

1990 – 1997

With the divorce concluded, Erik and Elissa ensconced in Idaho and Swen graduating from high school, my life took on yet another flavor.

SWEN

Swen had never been comfortable in school. He was shy, and penmanship was difficult, although it was becoming clear that his brain worked out math issues better than mine ever would. He created long and convoluted domino constructions in his room that were triggered by levers and weights to crash down when the time was right. He loved animals and insects. I had not encouraged him to take college prep classes because I didn't want him to suffer another four years.

One day, Jesse, Swen's best friend and our mountain neighbor who more or less lived at our house, came to me and said, "Laura! I am taking Swen to college. He's too smart not to go."

So much for my assessment of my beloved son.

Jesse was going to the Bay Area where he could live with his grandmother and attend Laney Community College. He did indeed take Swen with him. Tom and I visited them and inspected the attic where they both lived. We were invited to dinner, which was formally served each evening by the grandparents. The great-grandfather was present and also lived in this rambling Berkeley house. He was ninety-eight and the local Scrabble champion. He didn't hear much, so he sat and smiled, eating his dinner. I was very satisfied with Swen's new situation.

They completed a year there. Swen continued studying at community colleges in Santa Cruz, San Francisco and Santa Cruz again, and finally made it to UCLA where he enrolled in an engineering program suited to his excellent math skills. He wasn't much interested in being an engineer, but that was solved in a surprising way about the time he was to graduate.

Swen's girlfriend, Shannan, worked at Digital Domain, a company in Venice Beach that created visual effects for movies. She arranged a summer internship for Swen, and it seemed perfect for his talents. He could use the spatial engineering knowledge to figure out where the film would be shot and add or subtract the special effects. He was hired. He was in his last quarter at UCLA and ready to toss it, figuring he didn't need the degree because he already had the job. But I needed the degree for him!

"Wait a minute!" I shrieked. "It's not like I want to see the piece of paper," although I did, "I just can't bear to see you quit now after eight years of studying and losing credits from transferring schools. I will get up at the crack of dawn and drive you to your final classes."

I didn't have to.

He graduated.

He still works in the same field more than twenty-plus years later.

Gale

In the mid-eighties, Gale had decided she wanted to leave Malibu. She discovered Sandpoint, Idaho, and moved there with her husband, Don, and two teenage sons, Jeff and Mike. They built a beautiful home. The boys moved back to Malibu the minute they graduated.

I drove there several times after visiting Ruthann in Sun Valley, and later Erik and Elissa in Stanley. Sandpoint is sixty miles south of the Canadian border and was indeed beautiful. Six women from the Women's Council flew up, and we windsurfed—or tried to, in my case. And drank huckleberry margaritas.

Gale had been traveling to Monrovia where her mom lived to substitute teach and supplement their income. After eleven years in Idaho, her long marriage crumbled.

She called me in tears. "I don't know what to do! I hate leaving the home that I designed and the beautiful lake and my horse. But I just can't be with Don anymore."

"Well, Swen has gone off to college. You could stay in his room for a few months until you figure out what you want to do."

She stayed eight years.

I painted over Swen's day-glow orange-and-black décor with a lovely rose color. The first time he returned home he was mortified. "Mom! How could you do this?"

"Well, I didn't think your color combo would be to Gale's taste and you have, after all, moved out. Haven't you?"

"But this is still my home, isn't it?"

I felt horrible.

"I can tell you from experience, it is not good to move home again after you leave." I rememberied the disaster I endured at my parents after having lived in the dorm.

"Does that mean I'm not welcome here?"

I looked up at his big blue eyes that seemed close to tears. "Oh my God, no. I didn't mean that. Just that once you've gained certain freedoms away from your parents, it is hard to live together again."

We hugged and wept a bit. I explained how Gale could help me pay the rent and keep the yard up, since everyone else was gone now.

He seemed to understand.

WORKSHOPS

During most of the nineties, my house was a workshop haven.

I personally taught partner massage and later *Facing the Final Mystery* workshops. Tara taught how to use essential oils for healing as well as East Indian cooking. Tara and Myrna led many mask-making days, spreading out a plethora of decorative accessories on tables set up with plaster and mirrors. Franci came several times a year and gave psychic readings by appointment.

Most of these days were followed by pasta primavera dinners I cooked, or the results of the Indian cooking class, if Tara was teaching. Wine flowed, laughter burst forth, and everyone seemed to enjoy the companionship while absorbing the new information the day had provided.

Romance

Once I sent our family Mac off to college with Swen, I had to buy a new one for myself.

A woman at a retreat-planning meeting recommended a specific computer store and told me they would take care of everything I needed. I bought a new computer and printer and signed up for the classes they offered. The teacher was tall, pudgy with greying sideburns. I assumed he was in my age category. It turned out he was eleven years younger. He had a delicious voice, deep, and with a faint Floridian accent. He was very smart and also very funny. I was charmed. I signed up for another class. He walked me to the stairway leading downstairs to the parking lot. I was a-flutter.

We started seeing each other.

It wasn't easy.

I realized later I had fallen in love with the teacher-persona, who was only present in the classroom.

When he was not teaching, he was not very funny, and his social skills left something to be desired. He turned out to be a binge alcoholic and was tardy most of the times we planned to meet. There were sweet and tender moments, of course. I am not a masochist.

The relationship went on way too long. Nonetheless, I continued my dance classes, massage, girlfriends and trips to the ranch twice a year. I complicated it by appointing myself his assistant and worked hard making sure he got the schedules out on time so students could actually sign up before the class took place. He did not understand that simple task. Several years after we broke up, I visited him to get help with the computer he gave to me.

"Look at this," he said, motioning me to his computer. He pulled up a Quicken graph which indicated that the year I helped run the office had earned much more income than the year before, or after. I was pleased he appreciated that.

We parted amicably, although it took me months to complete the break. I hadn't wanted the management of his office to fall apart.

Mother Teresa syndrome, I guess. And yes, it did fall apart.

Tom reappeared soon after, despite his married state. We went camping and traveling up and down the coast whenever he came to town.

Titanic

A movie location business opened up in Malibu. Everyone I knew signed up, and photographers came out to create a portfolio of what our homes could offer. Years passed, and my house was chosen for a scene in "Titanic," the biggest movie ever at that time. They used my kitchen and screen porch as the setting for the scene in which the character Rose lives as an old lady potter, the one who was Leonardo's love interest as a young woman.

While the scene in the movie did not last more than a few minutes, Gale and I had to move out for two weeks. The crew brought cartons of accoutrements for decorations, shored-up the screen porch and built a cabinet over the ugly wall heater, which they left in place. I received a nice chunk of change, more than I had ever seen in once place. It allowed me to purchase new carpet and a brand new RAV4. I continue to drive it in 2019.

Circle of Caring

One of my nursing school classmates, Helene, told me about a wonderful weekend for nurses in Lake Arrowhead focusing on self-care. She told me all about it and gave my contact information to the director. Katherine called and invited me to participate by teaching partner massage and yoga at the weekend. The other group leaders, Shira, BJ and Katherine and I became like family.

I was honored and pleased to be with nurses again.

I taught at this weekend twice a year for the next twenty years.

Teaching at my Massage School

Around the same time, I was invited to teach a hygiene class at my massage school. I drew upon my nursing background and created a class that was interesting, useful and fun.

I taught it every few months for almost twenty years.

Facing the Final Mystery

1997 to the present

Our pal Viveka encouraged Gale and me to join her at Toastmasters. Begged may be a better verb. She was opening a new business and wanted to improve her public speaking in order to drum up new clients. She insisted it was a lot of fun, even when she told us that while giving her second speech she had to drape herself over the lectern while her knees shook and she had to concentrate on not throwing up. We didn't think that was such great advertising.

We certainly didn't need Toastmasters; we'd never even heard of it.

It *was* kind of fun. In fact, it was more than fun. It was the most organized system of knocking the public-speaking-fear out and away and getting rid of all those pesky *ums*, *ers* and *ya'knows*. After the meetings, we went directly to the nearest pub for a glass of wine and to parse the evening's activities. The watering hole was called the Black Angus, but the neon "g" was burned out, so our giggles were off to a roaring start each week.

Since I was only there to support Viveka, it came as a surprise when I noticed that six of my first ten speeches were related to end-of-life issues, undoubtedly a result of my stage of life. My mom, in her mid-eighties, was begging me to "bump her off" if she ended up a vegetable like her Aunt Alice. I kept telling her to drop that image and pray for a peaceful death.

A young friend of mine had a recurrence of breast cancer and entered the active stage of dying. Hospice was brought in, and I was invited to participate in the final days. I had never witnessed an at-home death, nor hospice in action. It was transformative.

I began reading and reading, trying to find out why death seemed such a scary thing for so many people, when it was the only sure thing that would befall everyone.

I attended end-of-life seminars and workshops and finally created my own daylong workshop. At a speaker's conference, I went to a mini-presentation on writing a book—the man said, "If you are going to teach a topic, have a book to sell."

Me? Write a book?

That was even further from my mind than Toastmasters had been.

I collected stories, poems and drawings from the workshops at my house. It was obvious that once people felt safe, they would express their fears and open their minds to contemplating dying and death in a new way. I must admit, my first draft, thoughtfully read by about ten friends, was a bomb. I had tried to scare people into preparing their end-of-life documents and got instant feedback, especially from Ruthann, who called it a "tome," and Hedwin, who sat me down and said, "How about if you…"

Back to base one.

A book did emerge, and I began speaking everywhere I was invited: Kiwanis or Optimist breakfast meetings, where most of the attendees were interested in bacon and eggs; monthly meetings of psychotherapists, who really did seem to understand the need to explore their feelings about end of life; gerontology centers at colleges, who surprisingly had their own issues and fears about this topic; and religious groups, who were more fearful than I had imagined.

It was a rich time. Once discussions began about death and dying, there wasn't much people would not talk about.

And I loved their stories.

Lois

1998

Once I promised my mom I would look into "bumping her off" if she really ended up in a comatose state—I wasn't planning on doing that, and I was working on the "pray for a peaceful death" aspect—she started preparing in her own way. She had her and my father's wills and advance directives in order and their cremations paid for, which was so helpful to me. She invited Swen and me to drive her and my dad all over Los Angeles to look at the places my parents had lived during their long lives. It was a great day. We ended up at the restaurant, Taix, that they had frequented since before I was born. My mom placed a sign on her fridge saying, "Jesus, I am ready!"

She called me one day and said she felt a funny fluttering in her chest.

"Do you want me to come in and take you to the doctor?"

"No. I'll take a little walk." She called me later and said she felt fine. She had had a mild heart attack the previous fall, for which she called 911, despite her alleged, avid desire to die.

The following Friday evening, Gale and I and our friend Mary Ann were sitting in the living room having wine and hors d'oeuvres. The phone rang. It was a police officer.

"I am sorry to tell you that your mother has died."

"You mean my father?" I responded. My heart beat rapidly and pounded in my ears.

"No, it's your mom. A lady on her floor checked on her because she hadn't seen her all day and found her on the floor."

"Oh. Oh, my. I'll be right there. It will take about forty-five minutes." Gale offered to come with me. We found my mom on the floor and thanked the officer for waiting.

I called the Neptune Society and lay down on the floor next my mother. She was such a mixed bag of qualities, funny and daring, but critical and bossy. I knew she would be a terrible patient in a nursing home, so I was somewhat relieved she had died, likely of a heart attack, before that became necessary.

When the Neptune Society arrived, they lifted my mom onto the gurney. Grief hit me for the first time. I belched out some sobs, confused by the combination of relief and loss.

During the following weeks, several of my friends helped me clean out the apartment. Her belongings were minimal, because she truly was preparing. I was grateful for that. Then they helped me orchestrate a lovely gathering in the senior residence where she lived. She had been the movie monitor for the building and was quite popular. Swen went to the nursing home, got my dad dressed in his suit, and brought him to the gathering. I'm not sure if my dad understood why we were gathered, but I know he enjoyed the cookies and coffee.

About a year later, I read *The Divine Secrets of the Ya-Ya Sisterhood*, a novel about daughters, their moms and the moms of their moms. It opened my heart to my mother and her mother. I cried and cried. It was one of those moments when literature saved my life. The story allowed me see my mom in a different light, as well as my grandmother. It let me feel grief that she was gone and yet would never be able to right the wrongs she felt about *her* mom. I was able to let go of expecting anything more from her, and finally understood she didn't have more to give.

One Last Trip to Denmark
1998

Because of dementia, my father was already living in a nursing home when my mother died. It took weeks for him to retain the fact that she was no longer alive after Swen and I broke the news. My dad continued to dial her now-disconnected phone number. I even received a frantic call from a telephone operator who was distressed by my dad's search for his wife of over sixty years.

My father was an unusually sweet soul. I had always had a simpatico relationship with him, and it continued during this last phase of his life. Weekly, I drove into Santa Monica and he and I walked to Izzy's Deli on Wilshire Boulevard. Living in the nursing home had cured his late-in-life drinking to excess, but he was particularly delighted that we had one glass of wine with our lunch. Over time, the waiter would spot us crossing Wilshire Blvd. and would meet us at the door with a tray holding two sparkling glasses of white wine. My dad's eyes would light up as if he'd won the lottery.

My dad was ninety-one by this time, and while his short-term memory was close to gone, he could still tell stories from his teenage years, when he had entered an apprenticeship as an auto mechanic instead of following his father and brothers into farming.

"You know, I taught many people to drive their first cars," he would say, beaming. "And they usually gave me coffee and cake or a beer when we got back home from the driving lesson." He shook his head slightly, smiling, remembering the feeling of being accomplished and rewarded.

During the following months, he regularly got my attention when he uttered, "Say, I'd like to make one last trip to Denmark." I humored him for awhile, hoping he would forget about that idea, but he persisted.

The idea for one last trip was not totally crazy. He had returned to his country of birth every few years since air travel became affordable in the fifties. Maybe he needed this trip in order to let go of his life on earth, which didn't seem a very pleasant one to me, living in a nursing home with squawking patients and coffee that was never hot enough.

I needed advice.

"Vera," I queried my eighty-four year old massage client as I rubbed her sinewy legs. "My dad keeps telling me he wants to make one last trip to Denmark. Should I take him?"

"Oh, Laura. For God's sake, take him to Solvang! He'll never know the difference!"

She had a point. Solvang is a quaint, faux-Danish village with rolling hills, windmills and bakeries. It's only two hours north of Los Angeles—a lot closer than Denmark. But somehow, I felt that would be cheating my dad. He really seemed to have a strong yen to complete this part of his life.

I put the plan in motion. I made sure it was all right with the nursing home to save his room. I wrote to our relatives to say we were coming. They were more than welcoming. I bought the plane tickets with the meager funds left in my parents' checking account.

The day of departure arrived. He didn't seem to remember about the trip, even though I had called to remind him ahead of time.

Red flag number one.

Nonetheless, he got with the plan right away. I gathered his clothes into a suitcase and dressed him. We made it to LAX in time to enjoy coffee and pie at a palm tree-decorated cafe in the international pavilion. This had been one of our favorite activities at the horserace tracks—Hollywood Park, Santa Anita and even Del Mar, reached by train. From the time I could get into the racetrack for free, by ducking under the turnstile, we managed several trips each year. Always, between the third and fourth race, we headed to the cafe for our pie and coffee. I wondered if he remembered this as we waited for our flight.

Once situated in the plane, I painfully recalled the crowded conditions of coach seating. I also learned that he needed to go to the bathroom frequently. On more than one occasion, I had to squeeze myself into the tiny bathroom to help him reassemble himself.

Red flag number two.

We made it to London where we had to change planes. I had no idea that Heathrow was the size of Texas. As we walked, and walked, we were offered a wheelchair, but my dad refused. "I can walk just fine," he said. He was indeed walking but looking more peaked with each step.

We finally made it to the loading area and sat down. Then he had to go to the bathroom again. I stood guard outside the door of the men's room and waited. And waited. Finally, I asked a young man entering the bathroom if he could check on my dad, who was wearing a red cap.

The young man came out of the bathroom. "I'm sorry ma'am. There's nobody in there." I started to freak out mildly, and wondered whom to ask for help or what to do. I then saw an airport worker pulling my dad along by his arm. The bathroom had a side door, and he had wandered off!

In Copenhagen, my dad's cousin, Gunnar, picked us up at the airport and took us to his home. My dad had been there many times over the years, so when he referred to Gunnar as Knute and told me he'd like to go home, I knew we were in trouble. Knute was an old Danish friend who lived in San Diego, two hours from Los Angeles.

Had the altitude and stress of the plane flight removed his remaining brain cells?

He seemed dazed. I was anxious for him and mortified for myself, thinking I should have listened to Vera.

In a day or two after resting, eating and sipping a bit of aquavit, a favorite Danish spirit, my dad perked up and began speaking Danish as if he had never learned English. Gunnar and his wife Betty took us to visit various Copenhagen relatives. They also hosted a lovely dinner party in his honor. My dad took a look at my cousin Jette's husband and said, "You look like Bill Clinton." Her husband did, indeed.

There were still some functioning brain cells!

We drove on to my cousin Peter's home in Aarhus—he was equally gracious—and then to Nørre Sunby and the home of my first cousin Else. More hospitality. Plus, she reported that my father had told her stories about her father that she had never heard. That seemed almost worth the trip. My dad now seemed very comfortable. I was a bit more comfortable, but always waiting for another red flag to fly. We finally made it to the north of Jutland with my cousin Helle, where my dad was raised. We were invited into the farmhouse where he was born, driving past the Ford dealership where he had done his apprenticeship.

Surely I was fulfilling his dream to revisit his early life and family.

One big challenge for me was that in every household that hosted us, the bathroom was either at the top of, or the bottom of, a steep stairway from where we slept. I didn't want my dad to navigate the stairs by himself, so I slept like a cat with one eye open. I am fairly sure I slept less than two hours during the two weeks we traveled.

Finally, after the wonderful Danish meals, conversations and sightseeing, it was time to return to Los Angeles. In each airport, I now explained to my dad that he needed to ride in a wheelchair so that I could put our bags on the chair. He agreed. Heathrow now became as manageable in size as Missouri.

I got my dad back to the nursing home and situated in his room. I somehow drove home and slept for two days straight.

The following week, I arrived to take my dad to lunch at Izzy's. After he greeted me warmly, he said, "Say, I'd really like to make one last trip to Denmark."

Leaving The Knob
1999

The research I was doing for my workshop and my book, *Facing the Final Mystery*, got me to thinking about my own financial situation and that it was time to draw up a will dealing with the disbursement of my belongings, meager as they were. I called a meeting with Carl and Chantal and explained my concerns.

"Here we are on Barney's Knob. Carl and I co-own the ten acres, and we can't divide it because of land-use laws. Chantal, you've put a lot of your money into creating new rooms in the studio and beautiful landscaping."

While I was quite pleased with how my side of the fence looked now, with its aloes, agaves and geraniums, their side was lush with bougainvillea, clematis and grape arbors. It remained lush due to automatic watering systems and hired gardeners. I wasn't jealous, but there it was: our financial combo was a mess.

"Do you have any ideas about how we can write this up?" I asked Chantal, after I explained my concerns about what would happen if or when one of us died and we didn't have a plan. Carl was slumped in a chair and was sporting his green tinge. He didn't like talking about death and dying.

"No. What do you think?" asked Chantal.

"Could you get a life insurance policy on Carl and then if he died, you could get your money back?" I suggested.

"If I died," I offered, "I would want Erik and Swen to inherit my portion of the property, so that is pretty easy, as long as I get it written down."

Despite my studies, I was still fairly naïve about the financial world.

She called me back in a few days, and with her cute accent reported, "He is worthless. We cannot get a life insurance because he smoke cigars!"

Was this true? If so, it was on to Plan B, whatever that was.

I described my concerns to Erik when I visited Idaho for Christmas. He listened, and we noodled various ideas. Then he asked, "How much money would you be happy to receive for your half of the place?"

I hadn't thought of that since the fateful day of the $15,000 offer and the pot-throwing incident. I was still very attached to my home and life on The Knob. I thought about his question overnight, and we resumed our discussion the next day.

"We paid $110,000 to the Griffins—a gift really. If they had not offered to sell it to us after sixteen years, we couldn't even have this conversation. It would be worth nothing to any of us. We've lived there for almost thirty-two years. Let's say it was double that price. I could leave with $100,000. But remember, I haven't even thought of leaving, just organizing my thoughts so we can write our wills."

"You sure?" Erik asked. "You know it's worth more than $200,000."

"Yeah, but we only came up with $10,000 down, which the Powells and their friends helped us acquire by buying big pots. Nothing really came out of my actual pockets."

"Okay. We can keep talking about it and see where it goes."

We finished our Christmas celebrations, and I drove home just before New Year's 1999.

A MONTH OF THURSDAYS

About a week later, I woke up—it happened to be a Thursday—and I heard a voice say, "You can leave, you know."

I looked around to see who said that prophetic sentence.

No one was there.

Was its my guardian angel, my higher self, or a dream.

I stayed in bed until I heard Gale in the kitchen making her coffee. She didn't like to hear about my dreams, or other ideas, until she was caffeinated.

It was winter, but not very cold. "Let's sit outside. I have something important to discuss."

We moved out to the patio, facing both the canyon and the ocean.

"What?" she asked.

"I heard a voice."

That got her attention.

"What kind of a voice?"

"I don't know."

By this time we were the woo-woo gals, so strange voices didn't freak her out.

"Well, what did it say?"

I told her what I'd heard. She had already announced she was moving to Boise at the end of the school year to look after her mom, who had had a stroke the previous fall, so I wasn't worried about making her feel homeless.

"Wow! That's interesting. What do you think?" she asked.

I told her about my conversation with Erik. "I'm not telling anyone about this except you, okay?"

A Consultation

I figured I could use some outside guidance and called Ron-San, my Vedic astrologer friend. I needed a New Year's reading. He drove out on his first available day—the following Thursday. We sat down at the kitchen table, and he spread out his astrology ephemeris and some books, glancing at my chart.

"Hmmm…" he said, about five times.

"Hmmm…what?" I prodded.

He turned more pages and continued with his *hmmms*.

Finally, he looked straight at me and said, "It looks like you're going to lose your home, or lose your attachment to your home. Or it could burn up. Or, you could just leave."

He waited for me to say something, worried I would be upset at this news. He had lived in the canyon for years and had helped us with various home improvements, like installing skylights and windows he had inherited from construction jobs. He knew how attached I was to The Knob.

Eventually, I said, "Don't worry about freaking me out. There do seem to be changes in the wind."

He continued with other areas of the reading, but these words stuck with me.

Tigger

The next Thursday morning, Gale asked, "Have you seen Tigger? He hasn't eaten breakfast, and I heard a cat yelling during the night."

We walked out onto the deck and looked around. Tigger liked to sit on the railing and peruse the canyon. We saw no feathers or fur, but we guessed that an owl might have swooped down and carried him off. Gale brought him to The Knob eight years earlier, and he survived, but was now probably fourteen or fifteen years old. She was sad. I was sad for her, and yet there was something about lightening our loads as changes seemed to be in store for us.

Trail Meeting

I felt a need for solitude and reflection. Another week had passed. It was Thursday again. I looked at the lot next door—the fireman who had owned the area had died and left it to his son, who turned out to be a pain-in-the-neck. He posted Day-glo orange "Keep Out" signs on the eucalyptus trees facing our side. We tore them off; he replaced them. He told us personally to stay off of his property, although aside from the flat area for the helicopters and a dirt road out to Decker Road, there was nothing to protect.

I looked towards his side and didn't see any sign of him, so I walked quickly across the flateau to the trail. I sat in the cave for about an hour wondering what could be ahead. Since the voice, I'd gotten used to the thought of leaving. I didn't know to where. I was writing *Facing The Final Mystery* and had started picturing a studio room where I could write and live on my own. It hadn't occurred to me that I had never lived alone. Parents, dorm roommate, husband and children, Gale—it was a bit daunting to consider, but also kind of freeing.

What might I do, or who might I become, without having to wonder about housemates?

I climbed up to the rocky ridge above the cave and gazed across at our compound. I could see a blue vehicle and figured the fireman's son was there. I decided to detour on the trail that opened out to the road. I came around the bend in the trail and ran smack into Carl.

He was alone.

He was never alone; he was always walking with Chantal.

We shared a brief hug.

"Where's Chantal?" I asked.

"She went back home because her parrot pooped on her shoulder."

Ah, ha.

This was the moment. Unplanned. Unforeseen. Unique.

"Carl, I'm thinking of leaving here."

He looked shocked.

"But...but why? I thought you were happy here, that we'd worked out a lot of things."

"I've been very happy here, but I think it's time. The boys are gone. Gale is leaving. I think it would simplify our end-of-life issues if you could buy me out."

He stood there quietly.

There was some way we had continued to look after each other, despite the marriage ending. It was nothing that we had ever talked about, though. It was something profound—maybe a connection from a past life.

We sood together in silence.

Yet again, perhaps there was something simpler operating: he might not like me to leave because he would have to rent my house out to someone who could cause problems because of his illegal kilns and lack of permits.

"Let me know how you can buy me out," I finally said.

We turned and walked together out to the road and ran into Chantal. When we got back to the fire station, I looked at our parking lot. The blue vehicle I had seen from the cave knoll was my own Toyota! I could have walked across the ridge easily, but I would have missed this moment with Carl.

Serendipitous experiences seemed to be guiding me toward huge changes.

Saturn

My cat, Saturn, was almost nineteen years old. We had never had a cat last more than a year or two, because of coyotes and hawks. Saturn was as black as night, and I imagined that kept him hidden as he prowled the canyon.

But he was starting to get a bit wobbly and was electing to poop in the house. It seemed he knew he didn't have the strength to outrun a predator while he was doing his duty.

On the next Thursday, he disappeared. Gale was away. When she returned and saw his food and water bowls were gone, she looked at me with a question, "Gone?"

I nodded.

The Offer

The phone rang. "Meet me at the gate," Carl said.

He presented me with a document that read some version of the following: he would pay me $250,000 for my half. He would give me some amount up front, monthly payments and a balloon payment in five years.

I had lived with Carl long enough to know he liked to pay the squeaky wheel first, and I was not planning on squeaking. His offer appeared to be way more generous than what I had in mind, while what I really had in mind was to be gone and done with it.

I talked to Erik about it. He was still concerned I would settle for too little.

I called Carl back. "I'll be happy with $100,000, but only if it's in one lump sum. And now, before I leave."

"It's a deal. My dad will loan me the money."

We planned to meet at the bank opposite my old boutique. It had been torn down, along with the Chinese elm tree, when new owners bought Pt. Dume Plaza. I was not especially sad about the boutique, but it seemed criminal to dig up such a beautiful tree.

We stood in the bank, face-to-face, and he handed me a check for $100,000.

"Thank you," I said, as if it were fifty bucks.

We hugged, knowing this truly was the end of a long phase of both of our lives.

I deposited the check, thinking we should've had a cocktail to acknowledge the deal, but I'm not sure we would've known what to say.

In July, after thirty-two years, I was gone from The Knob.

I haven't missed it.

After The Knob

1999 - 2018

Creating a New Life
1999 to the present

THE NEXT DWELLINGS

While I knew I was ready to leave The Knob, the transition wasn't smooth. Friends helped me move to a castle-like dwelling where I could hear the surf and walk a mile to Lily's Bakery. I forgot to notice the drunk and crazy landlord, and I left in less than a month.

My friend Roger suggested I stay at his home while he and his wife were in Hawaii. While there, I realized I could live like a gypsy—traveling with just my clothes, computer, a few books for my writing project and framed family photos that could sit on the coffee table—no nails or tacks. I was letting go of my need to have everything in place, an old habit.

This new freedom allowed me to approach Betty and Harlan, the couple who had invited Gale and me to stay in their guesthouse during the "Titanic "filming. They were both eighty-four. I had encouraged them to put their large nursery for sale and move closer to their daughter, and I hoped I could rent the guesthouse.

"Betty, what do you think of me staying in the guesthouse to help you sort and toss before you move and give you your massages. When your family comes to visit for the holidays, I can easily pack a few things and stay with friends?"

I could see she liked the idea of having my support as she went through her upcoming changes. Her husband liked it too, and I moved in.

ROMANCE

Settling into the beautiful guesthouse overlooking Zuma Beach, I reconnected with Ray. He had tried to reach me while his wife was dying after hearing about *Facing the Final Mystery,* but I had no direct phone line while I was moving. I knew his family because his daughters, Pash and

Renee, rode the school bus with Erik and Swen and later babysat for me. Ray had built a home on Decker School Road, a mile down our canyon in the nineteen seventies. While we met for lunch to discuss Lisa's dying process, we found we had a lot in common and spent a full day talking. Letters followed. I was fifty-six and he was sixty.

Who knows when and where love arrives?

That winter, I drove to Idaho with Ray and celebrated the millennium by dancing and watching the clocks change around the world, successfully. The next morning as he and I soaked in the hot spring pool, we watched a bald eagle circle over our heads. I took it as a good omen for my future, even though I had no idea what it would hold.

We discovered that Ray had printed many of the art catalogues for Elissa's mother, Josine, while she was curator at Barnsdale Park, and Cal State Los Angeles—another good omen for connection, I thought.

Ruthann and I caravanned as far as Alamo, on very snowy roads. She was on her way to visit her sister in Arizona, and I was heading to meet with Ray in Las Vegas. It was already clear we were together.

Betty and Harlan's nursery sold in the spring. Ray's housesitting arrangements also came to an end. We had called ourselves the "elegant homeless" and now set out to find a home together. We rented an apartment on Agoura Road, at the bottom of the mountain where both of us had lived for so many years. Our windows and front deck overlooked the same chaparral-covered hillsides as had our Decker Canyon homes.

My Book is Done - 2002

I finished writing *Facing the Final Mystery*. It was a great accomplishment for a non-writer. Bette and I had encouraged each other through the low points of writing our books. We walked hand-in-hand to the post office to mail the disc containing the manuscript of my book to the print-on-demand company. There were parties to celebrate, more talks and workshops to give.

I thought the first edition was beautiful, but when it was time to reprint it, my friend Susan Dworski suggested she redesign it. Then, it was really beautiful. I continued to promote the book and the importance of talking openly about dying and death before a crisis occurred.

Our Wedding - 2003

Our previous weddings had been small, family-only affairs. I was ready to celebrate. Ray and I hosted a wondrous gathering of friends and family on the beautiful Wright Land, atop the Santa Monica Mountains. All four of our children were able to attend, flying in from four separate states. We danced and shared stories and ate good food. Barbara Cameron loaned us her apartment in Todos Santos for our honeymoon, another first for us. It was a great time.

Lumps and Bumps - 2004

Bette told me she was having trouble swallowing. I did not like hearing this news because she had always been a smoker. I told her it could be GERD and treated with antacid medications. I didn't want to visit my darkest fears. Her doctor treated her for that, but I think he knew too and ordered a scan. The results were not good—serious cancer followed by surgery with many incisions and chemo. She lived with a feeding tube for a year or so. She was so brave through it all.

I noticed a lump on my neck. I knew it wasn't supposed to be there, but like a good nurse, I ignored it for some months. Once I started the diagnostic journey, the doctor who did the biopsy came into the examining room, drying his hands, not looking worried, so I wasn't either.

"You have some suspicious cells," he reported.

"Suspicious of what?" I asked, my denial systems kicking in and picturing pollen responses or some pesky bacteria.

"Lymphoma," he said calmly. "But nothing a little chemo won't cure."

He had no idea I believed chemo was poison and should be avoided.

I dreaded telling Ray who had already lost one wife to cancer. He was his usual philosophical self. "We'll do what is needed and continue living until we don't."

I drove to Idaho as usual that summer and found myself singing "And you will note there's a lump on my throat," while passing through fields of tall cornstalks. Ruthann came out to the ranch and she, Erik and I took a long walk. As we stood on the bridge overlooking Warm Springs Creek, I made my announcement, with shaky knees. I didn't want to ruin our vacation time together.

"It seems I have lymphoma and will need chemo." I blurted. Ruthann was stalwart and quietly put her arm around my waist.

Erik said, "Tomorrow, we will go see my homeopathic doctor in Ketchum," as if he was mentioning what we needed at the market. I had to repeat my news to Elissa when I got into the house. She thought the visit to the homeopath was a good idea.

The doctor was a gorgeous hunk of a guy with cowboy boots, a plaid shirt and twinkling blue eyes. He examined me, prescribed a passel of supplements and recommended I find a Chinese practitioner when I got back to Southern California. I felt relieved.

Erik, Ian and I went ice skating and then to lunch at the Yum Bowl. They dropped me off at a teahouse at the foot of Mt. Baldy while they did errands. I ordered something called White Clouds in the Far Mountains tea, which was served in a French press and rosy-peach in color. I wrote in my journal, "I have been Reborn with Dr. Freeborn."

When I returned to Southern California, further tests indicated I had a chronic leukemia (CLL) and not lymphoma. The good news: no chemo in the near future. Less good news, it was incurable.

I went to see Bette. I climbed up on her bed and said I had news. She listened to my story calmly. But when I talked her husband, Jim, a few days later, he said, "Bette has not shed a tear through her whole ordeal, but when I came home from work yesterday, she was sobbing. I was alarmed and asked her what was wrong."

Bette replied through her choked up sobs, "The dog ran away and Laura has leukemia!"

I found the Chinese practitioner. He was a fourth-generation master of some sort, muscularly as wide as he was tall. His very kind American wife asked me the questions needed to determine my health, or lack thereof, and the tea he would brew.

I answered her questions by saying, "Fine....No, that's not bothering me...Fine...or...No that's just fine."

Suddenly, the master leapt up and shouted, "Why you say fine, fine, fine? You not fine! You very sick!"

I started crying. I also agreed to drink the tea he brewed in his back yard each week, always following another interview, during which I tried to avoid the word "fine."

I did feel better and continued the protocol for almost two years. When I asked him one day, "How long should I continue to do this?" he replied, "Forever!" I decided that was too long, and I quit.

Bette died a year or two later, after grueling treatments. When I was driving to her home for the memorial gathering, The Beatles were singing, "She's got a ticket to ride."

I felt a pang of relief, knowing she was free from her bodily pain, even though I knew I would miss her terribly.

Swen's Wedding

2007

We were all happy when Swen met Wendy, a lovely girl who was both a DJ and an earth scientist. They were collectively known as "Swendy." He was in his early thirties and had had some good girlfriends, but never fell head-over-heels until he met Wendy. We all liked her.

Once they decided to marry, he asked Carl and Chantal if he and Wendy could have the wedding at the old homestead on The Knob. They agreed and all the plans started falling into place: the caterers, bartenders, table and chair rentals and a bus to bring guests down the long one-way driveway.

Swen called me. "Mom, there is something weird at Dad's."

"Like what?" I asked.

"Can't quite explain it, just weird. Dad asks a lot of questions, like where's everybody going to park. I tell him we have it handled, and then he asks something else."

"Swen, if you think they aren't behind this, let me know. I can arrange for the wedding to be where Ray and I got married." I had offered it earlier, but I understood his desire to marry where he had grown up from birth to eighteen.

"Okay, thanks. I'll let you know," he responded.

There were a couple more calls like that, but by that time the die was cast and the invitations were out.

I drove down from Oregon, and Ray flew south a couple of days later. I was staying at my friend Kate's in Topanga when my phone rang. It was Erik. He, Elissa and Ian had come down from Idaho for the wedding. Erik had been up on The Knob moving furniture to create the dining and dancing area.

"Mom?" His voice was quavering, not his usual deep baritone.

"What's the matter?" I asked, worried that Swen had gotten cold feet.

"Dad's got Alzheimer's."

Neither of us said anything for some moments.

"What?" I asked, as if I had not heard him. I just couldn't believe him.

If all the magazine articles were correct, in telling us to do crossword puzzles and learning new hobbies to prevent dementia, how could this happen to Carl? His brain was one of the most creative and well-used I had ever known. He had taught himself to make art out of every medium. He created glaze colors that needed chemical equations. He built giant kilns and the Paddle Cats. This must be wrong.

"Mom?"

"I'm here. I just can't absorb this. Can we meet for dinner?"

I drove down the canyon and we met up at the Reel Inn on PCH.

Once our dinners were served, we discussed this shocking news.

"Well," I said, "This may explain the strangeness Swen had been feeling when he was up there making plans. But, tell me what you know."

Erik cleared his throat. "Chantal asked me to sit down. She said they had known for almost two years but hadn't told anyone because they didn't want it to disrupt his business."

"Oh swell. So his sons may have missed two years of possible meaningful conversation because of Carl's business?"

It just didn't seem right.

"And what do we do about Swen? He's leaving for China two days after the wedding. Do we tell him before the wedding and make him a wreck, or wait until after he returns when Carl may be worse?"

We batted this issue around for awhile and finally decided not to tell Swen before the wedding.

I drove to Kate's and sat out on the deck overlooking the canyon and mountains on the other side. I determined to call Tom. I'd never called him at home since he married Debby, but I felt he needed to know this, plus I wanted his big-picture outlook. I couldn't grasp one. Debby had also been diagnosed with Alzheimer's.

Tasha was there and answered the phone. I told her the news. She had known Carl since she was five years old and couldn't believe it either. Then I talked to Tom. He was just as shocked. I was glad to hear both their voices and feel the connection with our long lives on The Knob.

The wedding took place without Swen's knowledge of his dad's condition. I sat between my two husbands during the ceremony. Carl looked frail and old, but still tall and handsome. Michael and Ruthann had flown in from Idaho and Patsy and Frank from Arizona. Boy-San attended with his beautiful wife and daughters. Many of the young people who had hung out at our house when Swen was in high school and college came. Some asked me to come over to our side of the fence with them so they could retell their memories. Our old house was being renovated and was gutted with no furniture, but the stories lived on. A lot of the plants were dead or dying, but a silver dollar eucalyptus tree Patsy had given me in a one-gallon pot was now about eighty feet high.

We ate and drank and danced.

Wendy's parents lived in South Africa and could not attend, but they sent touching toasts for her sisters to read. I toasted the couple and thanked Carl and Chantal for hosting the celebration. The grounds were beautiful and it seemed that all was well, especially as the temperature cooled off.

Ray and I drove up to Kate's and slept late.

Erik called the next day. "Mom, Swen told me that Chantal sort of backed him into a corner at the end of the evening and told him about Dad."

So much for our trying to protect Swen.

"What was she thinking?" I blurted. "She doesn't tell him for two years, and then not through the whole wedding planning months, and then she tells him at midnight of his wedding day?"

Erik was quiet. "I dunno. Weird as hell to me."

"How do you think Swen is with it?"

"I don't know. He was pretty tipsy by that time of night. He seemed exhausted and didn't know if he should talk to Carl before he left for China."

Ray and I headed back to Oregon.

I called Swen. "Swen, I know a mother is not supposed to call her son on his honeymoon day, but Erik just told me Chantal told you about Carl.

How are you?"

"I have no idea how I am. Wendy and I are just going to rest at home. I don't think I'll go up there again before I leave. Maybe I'll have a clue what to say or do by the time I get back."

Carl and I Talk... Sort of

2007

The following autumn as I was nearing Shasta City on my way to Southern California, my cellphone rang.

It was Katherine from Circle of Caring. "Laura, the retreat has been cancelled. There is an already-large and fast-moving wildfire moving up the mountain from San Bernardino. They think the Retreat Center is in its path and it could burn."

"Oh, my goodness! Again!"

"I hope none of the same guests were signed up for this retreat as the other one."

We had been in the middle of a retreat a few years earlier when we were called to evacuate at midnight. Several participants had taken sleeping pills and couldn't drive their cars. Some of their passengers couldn't drive stick shifts. While this was being figured out and everyone was packing their belongings, we were hustled into a caravan to get down the mountain safely. It was one wild and scary ride, driving toward flames on several occasions as we rounded bends in the road.

I was glad to learn of the fire *before* getting there!

Katherine asked, "Will you still come down?"

"I don't know. I'm going to get off the highway and figure it out. I'm not that far from home, but I've made arrangements to see my sons and all my friends. I have dates for lunches and dinners. Thank goodness I haven't passed the Oven Bakery in Shasta! I'll get a coffee and some yummy pastries while I decide what to do."

"If you do continue, let me know. I'd love to get a massage. I don't like you coming all this way and not being remunerated."

The semi-annual retreat had been my ticket for returning to Los Angeles to visit my sons and friends, since I had moved to Oregon. It paid for gas and set up a specific time for me to make visiting plans. Once I was fortified with coffee and pastry and had two loaves of the best bread in the world, I continued south.

Since the whole weekend was open, I called Carl and Chantal and asked if I could visit.

"Of course," Chantal said. "Come. We'll make a nice dinner for you."

I arrived and we sat in the living room. Carl sat across from me, quiet, but smiling. He looked about the same as he had at Swen's wedding.

"Carl, I thought it would be good to chat before I die from leukemia and you forget who I am," I said, feeling the truth of it, but also hoping it had a humorous ring.

He laughed.

I said, "So, I have this theory about Alzheimer's. It's completely unscientific, but it has been developing as I watch the people around me become forgetful, like your mom, and my dad, and parents of my friends."

He nodded.

I went on. "So, my theory is that if there is unfinished business that a person might want to forget, or, if something is too painful to remember, there might be a need to forget." I gave examples of my dad shutting down as my mom bitched at him in their final decades, and Carl's mom, who was terrified of running out of money before she died.

Carl reflected, "I think I know what you mean. I think that's why I repressed my feelings about my sister's death all these years. I didn't want to go there."

I almost fell off the couch.

It was the most insightful thing I had heard him say in the past twenty-three years.

"Yes, that's exactly what I mean! So, I wondered if there was anything you wanted to tell me or talk about, since we never went to therapy when we separated, or really talked about our feelings."

"Well, I think I just thought life was going on and I'd go along with it," Carl said slowly.

Just when I felt we were on a roll and were actually going to have a real conversation, Chantal interrupted, "Oh Laura, you always want to talk about the past. The dinner is ready. Let's eat."

She got up and walked to the kitchen. Carl stood up. I guess he was relieved.

I was devastated.

For the fifteen years after our separation, we never had the kinds of conversations, or murmurs, as we had called them, that I yearned for because Carl was fearful of Chantal thinking we were still connecting on some level. I understood this and respected it. But I thought that now, since I didn't live next door—in fact lived in another state—and had another husband, it would seem safe.

At least I understood that he understood and that we had connected on some level.

It was better than nothing.

We enjoyed a delicious dinner and I left.

I didn't see him again for several years.

Carl and I Hug... Sort of

2010 - 2011

A few years passed. Ian was a teenager. Swen was traveling all over with his movie work. Erik and Elissa moved from Idaho to Santa Cruz. Ray and I made new friends and gardens in Oregon.

Erik and Swen visited The Knob when they were in town, and kept me abreast of Carl's condition, which was deteriorating rapidly. He had fits of anger. There were stories of him getting up during the night and sweeping books out of a bookshelf onto the floor. His memory worsened.

Ruthann planned to visit my home in Oregon for the first time. She called and said, "I've got to cancel. Just had my third weird Pap smear. It's not Stage IV, but the doc says if it were her, she'd have a hysterectomy. I'm going to do that."

I was disappointed, but glad she was taking care of it. Her uterus was examined and appeared to be fine. The biopsies did not show cancerous cells. And then they lavaged her peritoneal cavity and found suspicious cells. Not just a basic uterine cancer but something with an acronym I can never remember, and which didn't have a good prognosis. Ruthann and Michael went to the MD Anderson Cancer Center in Houston, Texas. She, like Bette, was stoic and accepting of a treatment that was painful and long. When they returned to Idaho, she was cancer-free.

Tom called. I began chattering away about whatever.

"Laura, I'm sick," he interrupted.

"Sick?" I couldn't picture his bigger-than-life self as being sick. I had never seen him sick. He told me he had pancreatic cancer and decided not to undergo treatment because of the poor prognosis.

All of my important people were calling with bad news.

We stayed in touch on the phone.

I continued to travel south for the nurse's retreat twice a year. I was in

Malibu, on my way to Circle of Caring, and I called Chantal to ask if I could visit. She told me Carl had gone swimming at Pepperdine with Robert, a young man who was helping her care for him.

"Come over. He'll be home soon."

I arrived, and Chantal and I sat in the living room and chatted. She recounted that it was becoming more and more difficult each week. Carl could no longer swim a lap at the pool without Robert walking along with him to make sure his arms didn't flail against the ropes separating the lanes, tearing at his now-fragile skin. Carl had been a competitive swimmer as a boy and a master swimmer in his middle years. He still had the skills to swim, but did not know how to stay in a pool lane.

About a half hour later, Carl and Robert returned.

"Look who's here, Carl," Chantal gestured toward me.

Carl's face lit up like a child seeing his birthday cake or the tree on Christmas morning. He moved toward me with his arms out, wrapped them around me and started kissing my head all over.

We had not had this kind of physical contact for over twenty years.

I started crying.

I never understood why we couldn't at least hug during the previous decades. And here we were.

I was so grateful.

He was trying to talk but his words were jumbled.

Somehow, we separated and Chantal led him to an ottoman in front of the couch. He sat on it backward, facing away from Robert and me. Chantal got him turned around, just the way a mom would for a two year old.

It shocked me. But at the same time I felt a window had opened for a minute.

I didn't ask Chantal if he greeted everyone with such joy. I didn't want to know.

Was this our true selves coming together again for a moment? A final moment...?

Robert expressed curiosity about Chantal and my friendship, and we had fun telling him our various stories over the years when I lived next door—how the Mexican workers awkwardly backed away from us when they saw us chatting, and how Chantal's friends said they wished they could have continued raising their children together civilly, after a divorce.

It was time to leave. I stood and said to Carl, playing on the conversation we'd been having with Robert, "Carl, you were one of my favorite husbands!"

He stood up and grinned.

It took him a few tries to say clearly, "I was the best!"

We hugged again, and I left feeling exhilarated.

I pulled to the side of PCH overlooking Zuma Beach to sit and reflect on what had just happened.

Did it matter that it was one demented person seeing another with a vivid imagination. I knew what I felt.

Shortly afterwards, Carl was moved to a nursing home.

I never saw him again.

The Final Days

2012

FEBRUARY 2012

Swen's team was nominated for a Visual Effects Academy Award. He invited me to be his date. I protested, wondering what on earth I would wear. But as he pointed out, I was such a movie fan and it might be a once-in-a lifetime experience.

It was.

Patsy mailed me a dress that coordinated with the one pair of heels I still owned. We were treated to a luncheon, a fancy hotel, a limo and the post-Oscar dinner with Wolfgang Puck. We had a magnificent time.

I continue telling the story to anyone who will listen.

Swen continues to tell how often his mom tells the story.

MARCH 2012

Erik called. "I just heard from Chantal that dad has taken a turn. I'm driving down to L.A. and Swen is flying in, too." Swen had barely returned to Atlanta after the Oscars.

A turn?

"What does that mean?" I asked.

"Not sure technically, but maybe he had a stroke. He's unconscious and we're all gathering."

An hour later, the phone rang again. It was Tom's daughter, Tasha.

"My dad has taken a turn."

She used the exact same phrase!

I told her Erik had just called about Carl.

It was too eerie that Tom and Carl should check out at the same time.

"We've already been here in Colorado a couple of weeks because my dad has been so ill, but today, something is different," Tasha said. "We're expecting him to go pretty soon."

Tom died on March twentieth, 2012.

I learned later that Gina, my boss at the Hermes Project, also died that same March.

Carl died on March thirtieth.

During his last week, Erik, Swen, Boy-San and other friends of Chantal and Carl's, hung out at the nursing home. They called me periodically to report his changing symptoms. I relayed them to my palliative care nurse colleague, Mary Anne. "That kind of breathing indicates about forty-eight hours left."

She was right on the button.

Swen reported that watching his dad die was easy compared with watching him be fed while he was living in the nursing home.

APRIL 2012

Ruthann had said a few months earlier, "I'm in the endgame now."

I had to see her before the end.

I arrived at Ruthann's after a two-day drive. She was always tiny next to me, but now she was really tiny. She was wearing a knit hat to keep her bald head warm. We sat at the dinner table each evening and ate the meals her friends generously brought—except for Ruthann, who after savoring the flavors, had to spit hers into a cup because her GI tract no longer functioned. She was so brave and non-complaining.

One dies as one lives.

I watched her doing that.

After a few days, I hugged her goodbye for the last time and drove across the high desert to my home.

May 2012

Erik began planning a memorial for Carl to be held on The Knob. I gathered pictures from our family's life together. Chantal contributed photos from their years together. Erik placed them in a rotating file to be shown continuously on two computers at the gathering. We selected May thirteenth, which would have been Carl's seventy-first birthday.

The day before, we convened on The Knob looking at the photographs, telling the stories that went with them. Swen, Erik, Patsy and Frank were there. We all took handfuls of Carl's ashes and sprinkled them at the far end of the lawn, where Chantal said Carl liked to sit. It was a place he could see the ocean without my old house blocking the view.

The day of the celebration was sunny and warm. Ruthann's son David and his wife Amy traveled from Colorado to represent their family, since by now Ruthann was too ill to travel. People we had known for decades arrived, bringing food and wine. People stood and gave informal eulogies, sharing decades-old memories about the wild, creative, outspoken guy who was Carl Gillberg.

When I took my turn, I began, "I was barely twenty when I opened my front door to meet Carl…he was standing on his hands and I was looking at his knees…but I could see his elfin smile, even when it was upside down. I was hooked at that moment…"

How many times had I told that story?

June 2012

On June second Michael called to say Ruthann had died that morning. It was her sister, Brenda's birthday.

Erik, Swen and I joined Elissa and Ian in Ketchum for Ruthann's memorial in July. It was good to see David and Adam, whom I had known since they were born, with their wives and children. I was grateful to hug Brenda and thank her for helping Ruthann prepare for the end.

We drove over Galena Pass to the ranch for the weekend to reflect on all that had happened during this eventful year.

A bit of tequila helped.

I had purchased four Balinese flags in Topanga, one for each of my departed people. Ray made curved armatures for them so the puffy hearts attached to the flags would bounce in the air. Gazing at them that summer, I was inspired to tell their stories, which led to the stories of many other important people in my life, even though I couldn't include all the people I love.

Epilogue

2018

I had joined a writing group and continued working on the memoir. While I knew it wasn't quite done, I printed the first draft in October 2012 to send to my writer pal Trudy for comment and corrections.

On Friday, November 9, 2018, the Woolsey Fire started somewhere south of Simi Valley. The Santa Ana winds were fierce and the fire spread to the densely populated areas of Thousand Oaks and Agoura Hills. Total evacuations were mandated for tens of thousands from many communities.

The newscasters begin reporting, "This thing is not going to stop until it reaches the ocean." Barney's Knob lay on that pathway between the valley and the sea.

The waiting began. Swen had just returned to Venice Beach from Georgia. Erik had just returned to Santa Cruz from Idaho. I was in Oregon. We kept in touch. Emails poured in from friends who had spent time at our home over the decades. "I just heard Paramount Ranch burned." "The fire is burning homes at Malibu Lake." "I just saw fire engines parked at Decker School Road."

Of all the fires we had been through, this one was different. It was spreading faster and hotter and in many directions. The TV footage showed ridgelines in flames for miles, rather than moving through one canyon at a time.

Swen called Chantal that afternoon. They had not been in touch for a few years, but he knew she was alone on The Knob and might need help. She was, after all, his stepmother, although neither he nor Erik had given her that status. She had continued living on our plateau and had created a lively Airbnb business, renting out my old home and several other cottages and rooms she had decorated with Haitian art and landscaped entryways. It was a beautiful place.

Swen and Chantal made plans to drive up to The Knob to look around the next day, but PCH and Highway 101 were still closed. We all waited, tense and anxious without knowing if our ancestral home had survived. The winds had died down but were predicted to return on Sunday, possibly blowing embers and igniting unburned brush areas.

Later that afternoon, a friend of Chantal's managed to get past the barriers. He called her and said all the buildings were gone. He took photos and emailed them to her. We all began to absorb the stark losses. In one, seemingly untouched, there stood one tall, blue, curvy Carl-created urn amid the ashes and rubble. I thought it was both spooky and magical, as if Carl commanded to the firestorm, "You'll not get all of me just yet!"

We learned that the home Ray built in the 70s on Decker School Road had also burned to the ground. His first wife, younger daughter Renee and their husbands were living there. They and Chantal lost everything they owned.

While I was not suffering a personal loss of belongings or a roof over my head, I felt a mixture of sadness, nostalgia and relief looking at the photos.

Sad that the beauty of the plants, trees and all the sculptures and dramatic pots were gone.

Nostalgia at witnessing my entire adult life flashing before my eyes, starting with the barren plateau with the two scruffy buildings that turned into appealing homes for our family; trees that had grown from seedlings into tall pines and eucalyptus; all the stories that connected us to each other and our friends; the divorce, and creating our own personal gardens on either side of the fence as we continued our journey into adulthood.

Relief came from an internal feeling that something new and good would emerge. Already, Erik and Swen were reaching out to family and friends who had gone by the wayside. I knew from previous fires that nature would win out and the sage and chaparral would regrow. Wildflowers in the springtime following a fire were always voluminous and brighter. The flattened landscape was like a clean slate for new artistic creations and deeper relationships.

This was the final chapter of life on Barney's Knob as we knew it. But already, phoenixes were flying out of the ashes. It seemed fitting that just as I printed the first draft of my memoir, The Knob was swept clean.

I am not famous.

I don't know who will read these tales outside of my family and close friends.

But here is Barney's Knob, for whomever is drawn to the funny name...and a time and a place in a life.

Made in the
USA
Middletown, DE